LEGAL ALMANAC SERIES NO. 53

Legal Status Of Women

by

PHILIP FRANCIS

Oceana Publications

Dobbs Ferry **New York**

Library of Congress Catalog Card Number: 62-21448

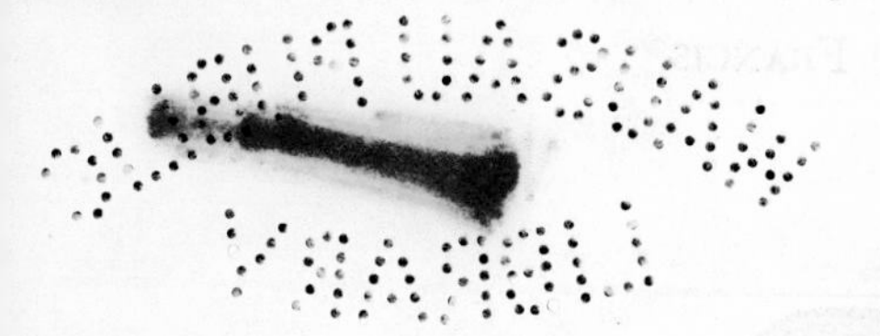

MANUFACTURED IN THE UNITED STATES OF AMERICA

TABLE OF CONTENTS

TABLE OF CHARTS

Chapter I

POLITICAL AND CIVIL RIGHTS

At common law, women's rights were greatly restricted. They could not vote, nor hold public office, nor serve on a jury. Upon marriage, a woman virtually lost legal identity as a person, as the husband assumed management and control of such property as the wife brought to the marriage, and the wife could not of her own right enter into a variety of business functions or agreements.

Today, however, it can be said of the role of women in American life that they have achieved equality under the law with men, notwithstanding the fact that certain practical discriminations are yet operative. Even in this area, rapid progress continues to be made, as women move toward achieving their goal of complete partnership with men in the economic, political and social life of the nation. And in some areas, it can be said to be "a woman's world." The generally earlier mortality of men frequently leaves women in a position of ownership and administration of considerable property. In fact, much property that is amassed during one's lifetime is frequently taken in the name of the wife. The result is that a substantial segment of American wealth and property is actually owned by women, a fact that has had and is likely to continue to have enormous impact on the shaping of our American society and institutions.

Citizenship And Naturalization

The Immigration and Nationality Act of 1952 eliminated the last discrimination against women under the immigration laws of the United States. The law now makes no differentiation between men and women in its application. Thus, it is now possible for alien husbands of American citizens to enter this country as non-quota immigrants, just as it had been previously possible for alien wives of American husbands to do so. In addition, a minor child entering the country may be charged to the nationality quota of either parent, rather than to the quota of the father alone; and an American woman, who adopts her alien husband's children may afford them non-quota entry into the country.

In the area of naturalization, a mother, equally with a father, if an American citizen at the time of the birth of a child abroad, may transmit American citizenship to the child. An American woman does not lose her own nationality upon her marriage to an alien, although she may renounce her American citizenship and voluntarily adopt the nationality of her husband. An alien woman who marries an American citizen does not automatically attain citizenship, but must comply with naturalization laws and procedures.

Voting Privileges

The Nineteenth Amendment to the Federal Constitution, adopted in 1920, prohibits discrimination because of sex in the granting of suffrage to citizens by any State. Under the American federal system, one of the powers reserved to the states is that of determining the qualifications and criteria for voting. The Nineteenth Amendment does not alter the states' position with reference to control over voting; it merely demands of the states that they treat women equally with men in applying the various qualifications—age, residence, literary requirements, etc.

Jury Service

Women are eligible for jury service in all except three states—Alabama, Mississippi and South Carolina; and in those states, by judicial decision, they are eligible to serve on federal juries, although excluded from state juries.

Twenty-four states have jury service laws which require women to serve under the same terms and conditions as men. They are:

> Arizona, California, Colorado, Connecticut, Delaware, Hawaii, Illinois, Indiana, Iowa, Maryland, Maine, Michigan, Montana, Nebraska, New Jersey, New Mexico, North Carolina, Ohio, Oklahoma, Oregon, Pennsylvania, South Dakota, Vermont, Wyoming.

Twenty-one states, the District of Columbia, Puerto Rico and the Virgin Islands permit women to be excused from such service on the basis of sex. They are:

> Alaska, Arkansas, D.C., Florida, Idaho, Kansas, Kentucky, Louisiana, Massachusetts, Minnesota, Missouri, Nevada, New Hampshire, New York, North Dakota, Rhode Island, Tennessee, Utah, Virginia, Washington, Wisconsin.

Eligibility To Hold Public Office

While under common law, women were greatly restricted as to political rights on the basis of sex and marital status, it is now true in all states that women are eligible for election to public office on the same terms and conditions as men. They are likewise generally eligible for all types of state appointive office. There are some types of offices, however, in which State law may require the appointee to be of a designated sex, i.e. offices in State penal or corrective institutions in which the sexes are segregated.

Women have been taking increasing advantage of the opportunities for elective and appointive office. In a recent article, Mrs. Alice K. Leopold, Assistant to the Secretary of Labor, Women's Bureau, Department of Labor, pointed to the following statistics:

> Sixteen women are serving in the House of Representatives and one in the Senate of the 86th Congress. They are members of committees which relate to international as well as to domestic programs. Their counterparts in state legislatures in 1958 numbered 311, and in 1959, 347.
>
> In the federal executive branch, women are serving as members of commissions and boards which help to determine government policies and as directors of agencies or divisions responsible for executing major programs.

State positions in which women serve in current administrations include posts in cabinets, as assistants and deputies to department heads, and as members of various state boards. Many women, likewise are employed by county and municipal governments in capacities ranging from chairmanship of a county council to town auditor.

Chapter II

CONTRACTS AND DEBTS

The Right to make Contracts

Under common law, the legal existence of the wife was merged into that of her husband. In general, therefore, the contracts of a married woman were void. Today, in every state, a married woman has had restored to her by statute many of the contractual powers that she lost under common-law rule, particularly in regard to property set apart to her as her separate legal estate.

New York State is typical of the completely broad base of women's contractual rights established by statute. In New York, a married woman may make contracts regarding property with any person including her husband, and she will be liable on those contracts as if she were unmarried. She has a right to contract for insurance on her husband's life. A husband or wife, however, cannot contract to alter or dissolve the marriage or to relieve the husband from his responsibility for support. A contract by a married woman does not bind her husband or his property, and a judgment for or against a married woman may be rendered or enforced as if she were unmarried.

Against the background of these general statements, it is useful to explore specific areas of contractual relationships:

CONTRACTS BETWEEN HUSBAND AND WIFE: Husband and wife may contract freely with each other regarding both real and personal property in 18 states. They are:

Arkansas, Colorado, Connecticut, Delaware, Florida, Idaho, Maryland, Michigan, Missouri, Nebraska, New Hampshire, New Jersey, New York, North Dakota, Pennsylvania, South Carolina, Utah, Wisconsin.

In 7 states, transactions between husband and wife are subject to the general rules that control the actions of persons occupying confidential relations with each other. They are:

California, Montana, Nevada, New Mexico, Ohio, Oklahoma, South Dakota.

In 5 states, there is a requirement that any transfer of personal property between the spouses must be by written instrument, and in some instances, acknowledged and filed for record. These states are:

Illinois, Kentucky, Mississippi, North Carolina, West Virginia.

Contracts between husband and wife are apparently prohibited in Massachusetts and Vermont, and restricted as to specifics in Iowa, Main, Minnesota and Oregon. The following states appear to make no statutory provision with reference to the right of husband and wife to contract with each other. They are:

Alabama, Arizona, District of Columbia, Indiana, Kansas, Louisiana, Tennessee, Texas, Virginia, Washington, Wyoming.

CONVEYANCE OF REAL PROPERTY: In 25 states, the wife may convey her real property as if she were unmarried. They are:

Arizona, Arkansas, California, Colorado, Connecticut, District of Columbia, Georgia, Idaho, Louisiana, Michigan, Mississippi, Montana, Nebraska, Nevada, New Mexico, New York, North Dakota, Oklahoma, South Carolina, South Dakota, Tennessee, Utah, Washington, Wisconsin, Wyoming.

In 15 states, a married woman's sole deed or conveyance transfers absolutely her rights and the rights of her representatives in her real estate, but has no effect on the husband's interest in her lands, unless he joins in the deed or conveyance. These states are:

Delaware, Illinois, Iowa, Kansas, Maine, Maryland Massachusetts, Minnesota, Missouri, New Hampshire, New Jersey, Oregon, Rhode Island, Virginia, West Virginia.

In 8 states, the husband must join with the wife in order to make a valid conveyance. These are:

Alabama, Florida, Indiana, Kentucky, North Carolina, Ohio, Pennsylvania, Texas.

TRANSFERS OF PERSONAL PROPERTY: In all jurisdictions except Georgia and Texas, a married woman may transfer her personal property to third persons as if she were unmarried. In Georgia, a married woman may not bind her separate estate by any contract of suretyship nor by any assumption of the debts of her husband. In North Carolina, contracts affecting personal property of the wife for more than three years must be in writing. In Texas, a wife cannot make a valid transfer of stocks and bonds owned by her without the joint signature of her husband.

Engaging in Business, Earnings, Wage Assignments

The right to enter into contracts suggests, as well, the right of a married woman to engage in her own separate business. In most states, as a result of statutory enactment, a married woman may engage in an independent business, using her own funds and acting on her own liability, without interference from her husband or others claiming through him. In some states—California, Florida, Nevada, Pennsylvania and Texas—statutes require a formal procedure on the part of a married woman who desires to engage in a separate business. This usually takes the form of a petition to the court of the county in which she resides showing why the common law disability should be removed. These technical requirements, however, are more honored in the breach than in the enforcement.

It follows from the right to engage in separate business

that neither spouse is liable for the separate debts of the other. Since a wife's earnings from her separate business are a part of her separate estate, these earnings are not liable for her husband's debts. Massachusetts provides, however, that a married woman, to protect her business from her husband's creditors, must record in the town where the business is conducted a separate business certificate. In Arkansas, California, Idaho, Montana, Nevada, Oklahoma, and South Dakota, statutes permit a married woman to place on public record a list of her separate personal property, from whatever source derived, in order that her rights of ownership may be protected from her husband's creditors. California and Nevada limit the amount of the husband's investment in his wife's business to $500, and in Nevada, the wife may lose the protection of the statute if her husband participates in the management of her business.

By the same reasoning, a husband is not liable for the debts of his wife arising out of her separate business. In Louisiana, the husband may become liable if the profits from the wife's business become community property. And in Massachusetts, if the wife has not filed her "separate business certificate," the husband may be found liable for her business debts.

EARNINGS FROM THIRD PERSONS: In the 9 community property states—Arizona, California, Hawaii, Idaho, Louisiana, Nevada, New Mexico, Texas, Washington—the earnings of a wife from third persons for personal services rendered outside the home become community property. Except in Idaho and Washington, the husband has the control and management of the wife's earnings along with other community property. In California, she may control community property money earned by her until it is commingled with other community property. In Nevada, she may control her earnings when they are used for the support of the family. In states where the husband manages his wife's earnings as part of the community property, he sues alone or, as in Arizona, joins his wife in the suit. It should be noted, however, that a husband cannot dispose of the community property with intent to defraud his wife. And the earnings of a wife living separate and apart from her husband are her separate property.

In all of the other states, statutes or court decisions operate to set apart for a wife as her separate property her earnings from third persons for personal services. These are free from her husband and his creditors, irrespective of his consent. These states give the wife control and management of her separate earnings, as well as the right to recover them in her own right. In Iowa, North Carolina and Pennsylvania, a wife may recover from her husband for services rendered to him beyond the scope of family and household duties, when a definite agreement or intention between them can be established.

WAGE ASSIGNMENTS: Assignment of wages—the promise of a wage earnier to pay a portion or all of his earnings to a creditor or other person—is restricted by law in more than half the states. In 16 of the states, the written assent of the wage earner's spouse is necessary to make the assignment valid. The states are:

Arizona, California, Colorado, Georgia, Idaho, Illinois, Iowa, Maryland, Michigan, Nebraska, Oklahoma, Rhode Island, Utah, Vermont, Virginia, West Virginia.

In 9 states, the wife's assent is required to an assignment of wages by the husband, but there is no requirement of the husband's assent to assignment of wages by the wife. These are:

Arkansas, Indiana, Louisiana, Massachusetts, Minnesota, Montana, Texas, Wisconsin, Wyoming.

New Mexico requires that the wage assignment of a married man must be recorded to be valid.

Exemption of Property from Seizure for Debt

All states have enacted some legislation granting exemptions of specified real and personal property from siezure and sale to satisfy the owner's personal debts.

WAGES: Garnishment is the procedure by which a creditor may reach the wages of a debtor. It is to be distinguished from the situation where a debtor voluntarily makes an assignment of his wages to a creditor.

The amount of wages held exempt from garnishment varies considerably among the states. In 20 states, wages are exempt if the money is necessary for family support. The exemptions range from all the debtor's earnings (unless the debt was contracted for necessaries or for personal services rendered by an employee of the debtor) in California, to $20 a week in Washington. The states are:

> Arizona, California, Colorado, District of Columbia, Idaho, Illinois, Kansas, Michigan, Minnesota, Mississippi, Missouri Nebraska, North Carolina, North Dakota, Oregon, South Carolina, Utah, Washington, Wisconsin, Wyoming.

In an additional 25 states, a portion of wages or earnings of a debtor, regardless of family status, is exempt. Such exemptions vary from a flat $15 a week in Connecticut to all wages for a 90-day period in Iowa. The states are:

> Alabama, Connecticut, Delaware, Florida, Indiana, Iowa, Kentucky, Louisiana, Maine, Maryland, Massachusetts, Montana, Nevada, New Jersey New Mexico, New York, Ohio, Oklahoma, Rhode Island, Tennessee, Texas, Vermont, Virginia, West Virginia.

The states of Arkansas, Georgia, New Hampshire, Pennsylvania and South Dakota have no specific provision for wage exemption.

PERSONAL PROPERTY: In 7 states, any personal property up to a certain value is exempt from seizure for debt. In the calculation of this basic exemption, wages, earnings and insurance are generally excluded. The value of property so exempt ranges from $200 in West Virginia to $2,000 in Louisiana. The states are:

> Florida, Indiana, Louisiana, Michigan, North Carolina, South Carolina, West Virginia.

In 5 additional states—Alabama, Arkansas, Ohio, South

Dakota and Virginia—a debtor is permitted to claim exemption of property up to a certain value, in addition to specified articles of classes of personal property.

The following categories of "personal property" are variously specifically covered:

Life Insurance—Except in 10 states—Arkansas, California, Colorado, Delaware, Georgia, Indiana, Massachusetts, Nebraska, Rhode Island and Virginia—all or a specified part of the proceeds of life insurance taken out for the benefit of the wife on the life of her husband is exempt from seizure by creditors. A fewer number of states have enacted a corresponding provision for the benefit of the husband as to insurance on the life of his wife.

Household goods—Except for those states that set a flat value on personal property exempt from seizure for debt—Florida, Indiana, Louisiana, Michigan, North Carolina, South Carolina and West Virginia—all states provide for some exemption of household furniture and furnishings in use by the debtor and his family. The amount of the exemption varies from state to state.

Wearing apparel—Wearing apparel of a debtor and his family is specifically exempt in 39 states, the majority of which exempt all such property, regardless of value. The states are:

> Alabama, Arizona, Arkansas, California, Colorado, Connecticut, Delaware, District of Columbia, Georgia, Idaho, Illinois, Iowa, Kansas, Kentucky, Maine, Maryland, Massachusetts, Minnesota, Mississippi, Missouri, Montana, Nebraska, Nevada, New Hampshire, New Jersey, New Mexico, New York, North Dakota, Ohio, Oregon, Pennsylvania, Rhode Island, South Dakota, Texas, Vermont, Virginia, Washington, Wisconsin, Wyoming.

Family provisions—Food and other provisions necessary for family support are statutorily exempt in 29 states. Massachusetts and Ohio place a $50 value on such provisions, while Wyoming exempts $500 of family provisions and household equipment. The states are:

Arizona, California, Colorado, Connecticut, District of Columbia, Georgia, Idaho, Iowa, Kansas, Louisiana, Massachusetts, Minnesota, Mississippi, Missouri, Montana, Nebraska, Nevada, New York, North Dakota, Ohio, Oklahoma, Oregon, South Dakota, Texas, Utah, Vermont, Virginia, Wisconsin, Wyoming.

Tools of trade—Specific exemption of a debtor's trade tools or his farm or professional equipment is made in 38 states. Statutes governing exemption of such equipment include professional libraries, office furniture, musical instruments and sewing machines. Generally, all such equipment is exempt. However, Wisconsin and Ohio set a $200 value and Oregon a $400 value. New Jersey exempts such property only if there are other goods sufficient for levy. The states are:

Arizona, California, Colorado, Connecticut, Delaware, District of Columbia, Georgia, Idaho, Iowa, Kansas, Kentucky, Maine, Maryland, Massachusetts, Michigan, Minnesota, Mississippi, Missouri, Montana, Nebraska, Nevada, New Jersey, New Mexico, New York, North Dakota, Ohio, Oklahoma, Oregon, South Dakota, Tennessee, Texas, Utah, Vermont, Virginia, Washington, West Virginia, Wisconsin, Wyoming.

In the application of these statutory exemptions, the statutes generally do not make distinctions between men and women. The emphasis in 26 states is placed on "head of a family," who is given a larger exemption than single person. In the other jurisdictions, no differentiation is made. Those states which favor the "head of a family," are:

Arkansas, Colorado, Delaware, District of Columbia, Florida Georgia, Illinois, Iowa, Kansas, Kentucky, Louisiana, Mississippi, Missouri, Nebraska, New Jersey, New Mexico, North Dakota, Ohio, Oklahoma, South Carolina, South Dakota, Tennessee, Texas, Virginia, Wisconsin, Wyoming.

REAL PROPERTY: With the exception of Delaware, District of Columbia, Maryland, Pennsylvania, and Rhode Island, all states have enacted "Homestead Laws" which have as their purpose the safeguarding of the family against debtors. These laws include those exempting the home from seizure for debt, restricting the sale or other conveyance without the assent of both husband and wife, and permitting a surviving spouse to continue to occupy the family home following the death of his or her mate. Where "homestead" is specifically defined, it generally includes the home occupied by the family plus outbuildings and, in rural areas, a specified acreage.

Persons entitled to exemption—30 states declare that the head of a family, i.e. a person on whom others are dependent for support, is entitled to a homestead exemption from seizure for debt by creditors. The states are:

> Arizona, Arkansas, Georgia, Idaho, Illinois, Iowa, Kansas, Kentucky, Louisiana, Massachusetts, Mississippi, Missouri, Montana, Nebraska, Nevada, New Jersey, New Mexico, New York, North Dakota, Ohio, Oklahoma, Oregon, South Carolina, South Dakota, Tennessee, Texas, Utah, Washington, West Virginia, Wyoming.

In 11 states, the exemption is accorded to property owners regardless of "head of family" status. These are:

> Alabama, Colorado, Connecticut, Florida, Maine, Michigan, New Hampshire, North Carolina, Vermont, Virginia, Wisconsin.

California and Idaho differentiate between heads of families and property owners, giving a higher exemption to the former. Minnesota declares that a "husband or wife" is entitled to the statutory exemption. A few states specifically provide that if a husband fails to claim the homestead exemption, the wife may do so.

To illustrate the various property exemptions—both personal and real property—as provided in a specific jurisdiction, the reader is furnished the following summary of the law in New York State.

The following personal proprety owned by a householder is exempt from seizure for debt: (*a*) Wearing apparel; (*b*) household furniture, tableware, cooking utensils, refrigerators, stove and fuel and family provisions for

60 days; (*c*) sewing machine; (*d*) family Bible, pictures and books; (*e*) radio; (*f*) domestic animals and feed; (*g*) wedding ring and watch not evceeding $35 in value; (*h*) tools and implements, including furniture and library not exceeding in value $600, necessary to carry on debtor's profession or vocation; and (*i*) church pew. These articles are not exempt from execution for a debt owed for work performed by a domestic laborer or mechanic, or for the purchase price (Civ. Prac. Act, sec. 665).

Where the judgment debtor is a woman, whether or not she is a householder, she is entitled to the same exemptions as a householder (Civ. Prac. Act, sec. 665-a).

Exempt presonal property owned by a man who is not a householder includes: (*a*) Church pew; (*b*) wearing apparel; (*c*) wedding ring; (*d*) watch not exceeding $35 in value; and (*e*) working tools and implements including furniture and library not exceeding in value $400 necessary for the debtor's profession or vocation. These items are not exempt from execution for money owed a laborer, mechanic, or domestic; or for purchase price (Civ. Prac. Act, sec. 666).

The earnings of a judgment debtor for his personal services rendered within 60 days before the action was begun, are exempt where it is established satisfactorily that those earnings are necessary for the use of him and his famliy if dependent upon him (Civ. Prac. Act, sec. 792).

The amount collectible under a wage assignment relating to any indebtedness aggregating less than $1,000 may not exceed 10 percent of the assigner's future wages in any month (Pers. Prop., sec. 48-a). No portion of the assigner's future earnings may be withheld by reason of any wage assignment unless such earnings amount to at least $30 a week, if the assigner is employed in a city of 250,000 or more population, or $25 a week if employed elsewhere (Pers. Prop., sec. 48-b).

Where judgment has been recovered and execution issued, ajudgment debtor may abbly to the court for an exemption of $30 a week if he resides in a city of 250,000 or more population, or $25 a week in other places (Civ. Prac. Act, sec. 684).

Life insurance proceeds payable to or for the benefit of a married woman are exempt from claim of creditors or representatives of her husband or her own creditors (Ins., sec. 166).

A plot of land with one or more buildings not exceeding in value $1,000, owned and occupied as a residence by a householder, designated as a homestead, is exempt from sale by execution issued upon a judgment unless the debt was contracted before the designation of the property or for the purchase money. No property is exempt from sale for nonpayment of taxes (Civ. Prac. Act, sec. 671). In order to designate property as a homestead, a conveyance stating that it is designed to be held as a homestead must be recorded (Civ. Prac. Act, sec. 672). A woman may designate a homestead in the same manner as a male householder (Civ. Prac. Act, sec. 673).

If the homestead exceeds $1,000 in value the lien against the judgment debtor attaches to the surplus as if the property had not been designated as an exempt homestead (Civ. Prac. Act, sec. 676).

A homestead exemption continues after the death of the owner for the benfit of the surviving spouse and children until the youngest child reaches the age of majority and until the death of the surviving spouse. The exemption lapses if the property ceases to be occupied as a residence by the person for whose benefit it continued (Civ. Prac. Act, sec. 674).

Chapter III

PROPERTY RIGHTS AND INHERITANCE

Interests in Real and Personal Property

Under common law, all of a wife's personal property in her possession at the time of the marriage vested absolutely in her husband. Intangibles—such as bonds, corporate stocks, claims for damage, etc.—belonging to the woman at the time of the marriage vested in the husband merely by the excercise of some act of ownership over them. While the husband did not acquire ownership of his wife's realty upon marriage, he did have a freehold interest in all lands owned by her with the right to possession and control during the marriage.

Under statutory law, however, a wife now retains the ownership of all property, both real and personal belonging to her at the time of marriage, and statutes have been enacted in all states giving her the right to acquire property which she may hold as her separate estate. As previously noted, it is generally true that neither the separate property of a married woman nor its income or profit becomes subject to the husband's debts. As a rule, neither spouse is liable for the debts of the other incurred before marriage, and each spouse is liable for his or her own debts contracted before or after marriage.

In the area of property acquired by joint efforts of husband and wife, the applicable legal picture is somewhat more complicated. In the non-community property states, property acquired by the husband and wife during marriage is generally under the management and control of the husband. However, the states have imposed statutory restrictions on disposition and use of certain types of property.

All states recognize joint ownership of both real and personal property. In fact, this system is widely used by husbands and wives with respect to bank accounts, securities, furniture, automobile and real property ownership since it protects the interests of the other if one of the spouses dies or becomes legally incapacitated. Because the legal implications are very different, it is worthwhile to explore the various methods of joint ownership.

TENANCY BY THE ENTIRETY: This was the common law form of joint ownership, which still prevails in Arkansas, Delaware, Massachusetts, Missouri, Vermont and Wyoming. The estate can be terminated or mortgaged during marriage only by the joint action of the husband and wife. Such an estate is liable for the joint debts of husband and wife only, but the rights of survivorship of the husband and his right to possession and enjoyment of the profits of land held by the entirety are liable for his debts. At the death of either, the property belongs outright to the surviving spouse.

In an additional 11 states, a joint ownership will be presumed to be by the entirety, unless the deed or instrument establishing the estate clearly expresses a contrary intention. These states are:

District of Columbia, Florida, Indiana, Maryland, Michigan, New Jersey, New York, North Carolina, Oregon, Pennsylvania, Tennessee.

TENANCY IN COMMON: This is an interest in land by two or more persons who hold such interest by separate and distinct titles, each party being entitled to an undivided interest in the property. Each party may dispose of his interest without the assent of the other tenants, and at death, the interest of such a party descends to his heirs or assigns, not to the surviving tenants. In Kentucky, Mississippi, Rhode Island, Utah and Virginia, a conveyance to husband and wife is presumed to create a tenancy in common, unless a contrary intention to create either a tenancy by entirety or a joint tenancy is clearly expressed. In 15 additional states, a tenancy in common is presumed unless an intent to create a joint tenancy is shown. These states are:

> Alabama, Colorado, Connecticut, Iowa, Kansas, Maine, Minnesota, Montana, Nebraska, New Hampshire, North Dakota, Oklahoma, South Carolina, South Dakota, West Virginia.

Georgia, Illinois and Ohio rule that a husband and wife may hold property only as tenants in common.

JOINT TENANCY: This is an interest in land held by several persons. Each has the right to dispose of his interest without the assent of the others. On the death of one of the parties in interest, the survivor or survivors succeed to the estate. Only in Wisconsin are husband and wife limited to joint tenancy as the method by which they may hold real property.

In 9 states, there exists a system of property ownership known as "community property." The states are:

> Arizona, California, Hawaii, Idaho, Louisiana, Nevada, New Mexico, Texas, Washington.

Under this system of law, the property acquired by the husband and wife, or by either of them during the marriage, otherwise than by ways which clearly suggest "separate property," is community property. The general rule in community property states is that the husband is the head of the "community" and the duty is his to manage the property for the benefit of his wife and family. Usually, as long as the husband is capable of managing the community, the wife has no power of control over it and, acting alone, cannot contract debts chargeable against it. However, in Arizona, California, Hawaii, Idaho, New Mexico and Washington, the wife must join in a conveyance of real property which is part of the community. In Louisiana, the husband may convey real property alone unless it is in the wife's name, in which case, she must give her written consent. In Nevada, the wife must join in a conveyance of the homestead. In Texas, the husband has sole power of disposition of both real and personal property.

Although briefly discussed in connection with property protected against creditors, the concept of the "homestead" has additional important implications for both husband and wife. The husband is usually given the right to select the homestead, although the wife may be so empowered where the husband fails to do so. It may be selected from the property of either spouse or from the common property of the marriage. After the homestead has been declared, 32 states require that consent of both husband and wife is required before it can be validly conveyed or sold, notwithstanding that ownership may be in one spouse. The states are:

> Alabama, Arizona, Arkansas, California, Colorado, Hawaii, Idaho, Illinois, Iowa, Kansas, Kentucky, Michigan, Minnesota, Mississippi, Montana, Nebraska, Navada, New Hampshire, New Jersey, New Mexico, North Carolina, North Dakota, Ohio, Oklahoma, South Carolina, Tennessee, Texas, Utah, Vermont, Washington, Wyoming.

In California, Hawaii, Idaho, Nevada and Washington, there are formal procedures set out for abandonment of the family homestead, and Iowa provides that if the owner of a homestead changes its limits or vacates it, such action does not affect the rights of the owner's spouse or children if it was done without his or her concurrence.

The surviving spouse has a vested interest in the homestead on the death of the husband or wife. The interest may consist of absolute ownership (California, Colorado, Kansas, Vermont, Wyoming) or a life interest (Connecticut, Illinois, Nebraska, New Hampshire, North Dakota, Oklahoma, South Dakota, Texas). In all cases, the interest is protected from creditors up to the amount set forth by statute (See Chart which follows). In community property states, where a homestead was not selected before the death of a spouse, the court will usually set aside a "probate homestead" for the benefit of the surviving husband or wife.

In addition to the protection against creditors, the survivor retains the right of homestead even though the decedent died with a Will which attempted to dispose of it. In such an instance the surviving spouse can elect against the Will and so take the homestead.

In states where the surviving spouse is entitled to dower or curtesy, the right of homestead is sometimes considered a part of the dower or curtesy interest, while in other states where the spouse takes as heir under the laws of inheritance, the homestead is in addition to any other share allowed by statute

The following chart illustrates the limit of value and area of the homestead in the several states. A few of our states, such as Florida and Kansas, do not place a limit on the value of the homestead, although the acreage may be limited. In Kansas the statute defines a homestead as 160 acres without, or of one acre lying within, the limits of an incorporated city which is used as a residence at the time of one spouse's death (Gen. Stat. §59-401).

Homestead

State	Limit of Value	Limit of Area
ALABAMA	$6,000	160 acres
ARIZONA	$4,000	None
ARKANSAS	$2,500	1 acre in city, town or village; 100 acres elsewhere
CALIFORNIA	$7,500	None
COLORADO	$5,000	None
CONNECTICUT	$1,000	None
DELAWARE	No law	—
DISTRICT OF COLUMBIA	No law	—
FLORIDA	None	½ acre in city or town; 160 acres elsewhere
GEORGIA	$500	50 acres outside of town or city
IDAHO	$5,000	None
ILLINOIS	$1,000	None
INDIANA	No law	—

State	Limit of Value	Limit of Area
IOWA	$500	½ acre in city or town; 40 acres elsewhere
KANSAS	None	1 acre in city or town; 60 acres elsewhere
KENTUCKY	$1,000	None
LOUISIANA	$4,000	160 acres
MAINE	$1,000	None
MARYLAND	No law	—
MASSACHUSETTS	$4,000	None
MICHIGAN	$2,500	1 lot in city, town or village; 40 acres elsewhere
MINNESOTA	None	⅓ acre in city, village or borough over 5,000 population; ½ acre if less than 5,000 population; 80 acres elsewhere
MISSISSIPPI	$5,000	160 acres
MISSOURI	$1,500 in country $3,000 in city	160 acres in country; 30 sq. rods to 5 acres in city (depending on population)
MONTANA	$2,500	¼ acre in city or town; 320 acres of agricultural land
NEBRASKA	$2,000	2 lots in city or village; 160 acres in country
NEVADA	$10,000	None
NEW HAMPSHIRE	$1,000	None
NEW JERSEY	$1,000	None
NEW MEXICO	$1,000	None
NEW YORK	$1,000	None
NORTH CAROLINA	$1,000	None
NORTH DAKOTA	$25,000 in town No limit in country.	2 acres in town; 160 acres in country
OHIO	$1,000	None
OKLAHOMA	$5,000	160 acres if rural
OREGON	$5,000	1 block in city; 160 acres elsewhere
PENNSYLVANIA	No law	—
RHODE ISLAND	No law	—
SOUTH CAROLINA	$1,000	None

State	Limit of Value	Limit of Area
SOUTH DAKOTA	$5,000	1 acre in town; 160 acres in country
TENNESSEE	$1,000	None
TEXAS	$5,000	200 acres in country
UTAH	$2,000 plus $750 for wife and $300 for each other member	None
VERMONT	$1,000	None
VIRGINIA	$2,000	None
WASHINGTON	$6,000	None
WEST VIRGINIA	$1,000	None
WISCONSIN	$5,000	40 acres of agricultural land; ¼ acre otherwise
WYOMING	$2,500	None

Rights Of Surviving Spouse

At common law the surviving spouse had a right of **dower** or **curtesy** in the real property of the deceased spouse. The surviving wife's dower right consisted of a one-third interest for life in all the real property owned by the husband during his life. Curtesy was the right of the husband to life estate in all of the deceased wife's real property. The life estate which is taken consists of the use and enjoyment of real property for the duration of the recipient's life; including all rents and profits which are derived from the land. This interest can usually be sold or assigned subject always to termination on the death of the original recipient.

Dower and curtesy attach to any property which the spouse owned at any time during the marriage, whether or not such property was conveyed by deed. The right is usually barred, however, where both husband and wife join in a conveyance of the property.

DOWER: Under our present statutes many variations of the common law right of dower exist. In some states the right has been completely abolished, while in others statutory substitutions or modification have been enacted. Certain requirements are necessary for a widow to be entitled to dower namely: (1) Lawful marriage; (2) The husband was possessed of an estate of inheritance in property, i.e., he owned a real property interest; and (3) The wife must survive the husband. Although the requirements are derived from common law they have usually been incorporated in the statutes of those states which have retained the dower right.

Under certain circumstances the right of dower may be defeated. The wife can release her right by joining in the conveyance of the property by her husband or by a property settlement between the husband and wife. The right of dower is usually barred where the wife abandons her husband without just cause or is divorced because of her adultery or other misconduct. Condemnation proceedings, which is the lawful taking of property by the state or local government, usually bars dower. The dower right always terminates on the death of the widow.

CURTESY: The common law right of curtesy has been abolished either expressly or impliedly in a majority of the states. As a substitute many states provide an interest for the husband similar to the dower interest granted to the wife.

The common law requirements for curtesy are as follows: (1) Lawful marriage; (2) Wife owned an estate or interest in real property which could pass by inheritance; and (3) Birth of a child capable of inheriting. The requirements are historical and have been modified in most states, where any form of the curtesy interest exists.

Where the right of curtesy or dower has been abolished or is unknown, the survivor usually takes as an heir of the deceased spouse under the laws of inheritance.

The following chart will illustrate the right of the surviving husband and wife in the real property of the deceased spouse. In the majority of cases, the interest which the surviving spouse takes is in addition to the rights of inheritance as an heir. In order to properly ascertain the complete rights of inheritance of the surviving spouse it is necessary to read the following charts in connection with the succeeding section on spouse's right of election.

Right of Dower, Curtesy and Statutory Substitutions

State	Husband	Wife
ARIZONA	None	Life estate in ⅓ of husband's real property if husband survived by lineal descendants and life estate in ½ if not survived by lineal descendants. (T. 34 §41)
ARKANSAS	Abolished Life estate in ⅓ of wife's real property (see footnote 1) (§61-228)	Abolished Life estate in ⅓ of husband's real property (§61-206)
CALIFORNIA	None (Civil Code §173)	None (Civil Code §173)
COLORADO	Abolished (ch. 176 §1)	Abolished (ch. 176 §1)
CONNECTICUT	None (see footnote 2)	None (see footnote 2)
DELAWARE	Life estate in ½ of wife's real property if husband survived by issue and life estate in all real property if no issue survive. (§3731)	Life estate in ½ husband's property, if wife survived by issue; and life estate in all if no issue survive. (§3731)
DISTRICT OF COLUMBIA	Life estate in all wife's real property (§18-215)	Life estate in ⅓ of husband's real property (§18-202)
FLORIDA	Abolished	One-third of all real and personal property absolutely (§731.34)
GEORGIA	None (§85-608)	Life estate in ½ husband's real property (§31-101)

State	Husband	Wife
IDAHO	Abolished (§32-915)	None (§32-915)
ILLINOIS	Life estate in ⅓ wife's real property (sh. 3 §170)	Life estate in ⅓ husband's real property (ch. 3 §170)
INDIANA	Abolished (§6-2353)	Abolished §6-2353)
IOWA	One-third in value of all wife's real property (see footnote 3) (§636.5)	One-third in value of all husband's real property (see footnote 3) (§636.5)
KANSAS	One-half absolutely, of all wife's real property (§59-505)	One - half absolutely, of all husband's real property. (§59-505)
KENTUCKY	Life estate is ⅓ wife's real property (§392.020)	Life estate in ⅓ husband's real property (§392.020)
LOUISIANA	None	None
MAINE	Abolished (ch. 156 §8)	Abolished (ch. 156 §8)
MARYLAND	Life estate in ⅓ wife's real property (art. 45 §7)	Life estate in ⅓ husband's real property (art. 45 §7)
MASSACHUSETTS	Life estate in ⅓ wife's real property (ch. 189 §1)	Life estate in ⅓ husband's real property (ch. 189 §1)
MICHIGAN	None	Life estate in ⅓ husband's real property (§558.1)
MINNESOTA	Abolished (§519.09)	Abolished (§519.09)
MISSISSIPPI	Abolished (§453)	Abolished (§453)
MISSOURI	Life estate in ⅓ wife's real property (§469.010)	Life estate in ⅓ husband's real property (§469.010)
MONTANA	None (§5812)	Life estate in ⅓ husband's real property (§22-101)
NEBRASKA	Abolished (§30-104)	Abolished (§30-104)

State	Husband	Wife
NEVADA	Abolished (§3361)	Abolished (§3361)
NEW HAMPSHIRE	Life estate in all real property of wife (ch. 359 §9)	Life estate in ⅓ husband's real property (ch. 359 §3)
NEW MEXICO	None (§31-123)	None (§31-123)
NEW JERSEY	Life estate in ½ real property (T. 3A §35-2)	Life estate in ½ husband's real property (T. 3A §35-1)
NEW YORK	Abolished (R.P.L. §189)	Abolished (see footnote 4) (R.P.L. §190)
NORTH CAROLINA	Life estate in all real property of wife (§52-16)	Life estate in ⅓ husband's real property (§30-4)
NORTH DAKOTA	Abolished (§56-0102)	Abolished (§56-0102)
OHIO	Life estate in ⅓ of wife's real property (§10502-1)	Life estate in ⅓ of husband's real property (§10502-1)
OKLAHOMA	Abolished (T. 84 §214)	Abolished (T. 84 §214)
OREGON	Life estate in ½ of wife's real property (§17-401)	Life estate in ½ of husband's real property (§17-401)
PENNSYLVANIA	None (T. 20 §1.5(a))	None (T. 20 §1.5 (b))
RHODE ISLAND	Life estate in all wife's real property (ch. 566 §12)	Life estate in ⅓ of husband's real property (ch. 418 §1)
SOUTH CAROLINA	Abolished (§19-101)	Life estate in ⅓ of husband's real property (4 S. C. 37)
SOUTH DAKOTA	Abolished (§56.0103)	Abolished (§56.0103)
TENNESSEE	Life estate in all wife's real property (see footnote 5)	Life estate in ⅓ of husband's real property (§8351)
TEXAS	None	None

State	Husband	Wife
UTAH	Abolished (74-4-9)	One-third, in value, of all husband's real property (74-4-3)
VERMONT	One-third in value of wife's real property (see footnote 6) (§3040)	One-third in value of husband's real property (see footnote 6) (§3027)
VIRGINIA	Life estate in all wife's real property except if issue survive then entitled to life estate in ⅓. (§64-20)	Life estate in all husband's real property except if issue survive then entitled to life estate in ⅓ (§64-27)
WASHINGTON	Abolished (§11.04.060)	Abolished (§11.04.060)
WEST VIRGINIA	Life estate in ⅓ of wife's real property (§4096)	Life estate in ⅓ of husband's real property (§4096)
WISCONSIN	Life estate in ⅓ of property owned by wife at death (§233.23)	Life estate in ⅓ of husband's real property (§233.01)
WYOMING	Abolished (§6-2501)	Abolished (§6-2501)

Footnotes

(1) Husband's interest may be defeated by will or conveyance by his wife. (§61-292)

(2) No dower or curtesy where marriage took place after April 20, 1877. (§7307)

(3) The survivor's share cannot be defeated by Will without consent. (§636.21)

(4) Wife takes a life estate in ⅓ husband's real property if marriage and ownership of property took place prior to September 1, 1930. (R.P.L. §190)

(5) Issue of marriage must be born alive. (§8098)

(6) Surviving spouse entitled to ½ in value of the real property if decedent was survived by issue or heir by adoption. (§§3037, 3040)

Dower and curtesy or the statutory equivalents thereof are property rights which grow out of the marital relation. On the death of a husband or wife, the property which forms the estate of the deceased descends or is distributed according to the laws of inheritance. In the states where dower or curtesy exists all rights of inheritance are subject to such rights of the surviving spouse.

At common law, real estate did not descend to the surviving spouse, but only to the heirs of the deceased. The right to any real estate of the deceased existed only by virtue of the right of dower or curtesy. To a limited extent, the surviving spouse shared in the personal property.

The surviving spouse in many states has a right of inheritance in the estate of the deceased in addition to any dower or curtesy right. The right of inheritance is statutory as the spouse is not strictly speaking, the heir or next of kin of the decedent. The amount or share which the spouse takes is usually dependent on the number of children or their descendants who survive and also whether or not the deceased was survived by parents, brothers or sisters or their descendants.

Some jurisdictions provide for an inheritance as an alternative to dower or curtesy, the spouse being required to elect. Where dower and curtesy no longer exist, the spouse usually takes under the laws of inheritance, which provide for the descent and distribution of all real and personal property.

The question arises as to the distinction between the case where the spouse receives a dower or curtesy share plus an interest in the estate under the laws of inheritance, and the case where only an interest under the laws of inheritance is taken and no right of dower or curtesy exists. The right of dower or curtesy is an interest in real property, which may be defeated or barred. The right cannot usually be defeated by the mere conveyance of the property by one spouse alone. It is an interest which is inchoate during the lifetime of both, and accrues absolutely on the death of the spouse. The right to take under the laws of inheritance, on the other hand, accrues on the death of the spouse, and only affects such property which was owned by the decedent at his death, subject to certain rights and liabilities as outlined by the statutes.

With reference to the rights of the surviving spouse in the several states, it must be noted that the share taken under the laws of inheritance is usually in addition to any right of dower or curtesy if such right exists, unless the statute provides that an election between the share must be made. Where the rights of the surviving spouse are dependent on the existence of issue or lineal descendants, the statutes usually construe the words to mean any children, grand-children, great-grand children, etc, down the line of direct lineal descendants.

RIGHT OF ELECTION: a. **Dower or Curtesy and Intestate Share:** Under many statutes which allow dower or curtesy, the spouse is granted the right to elect between the share taken by dower or curtesy and a certain distributive or intestate share. The statutes provide which share shall be taken, if an election is not made; the time within which the election must be made varies from state to state. The election must generally be exercised by the surviving spouse, during his or her lifetime.

b. **Election Between Will and Distributive Share:** Neither spouse may disinherit the other, in most states. Where one spouse dies leaving a Will which fails to provide for the survivor in any way, or provides a lesser amount than would have been taken had the testator died without a Will, the survivor may take the property under the Will or exercise a right of election. The right of election permits the survivor to elect to take the distributive share provided by law, as against that which would have been taken under the Will.

In some states the surviving husband has no right of election, while the widow may elect; many states allow either spouse the right to elect, although the shares taken may be different. In states where common law dower or curtesy or their statutory substitute has been retained, a testator cannot defeat by Will the share which the survivor would take. In some states the surviving spouse takes a share in the personal property in addition to dower or curtesy; while other states provide for intestate share to the survivor.

The prohibition against disinheritance by a testator is

not absolute, even in states where the spouse has a right of election. The misconduct of the surviving spouse may effectively bar the right of election. In Connecticut, abandonment continuing to the time of the testator's death, without sufficient cause, results in a forfeiture of the statutory share of inheritance. Adultery, desertion or failure to support may also result in a forfeiture.

Statutes usually provide a fixed period of time during which the election must be made. The right to elect is a personal right, however, and must be exercised by the surviving spouse during his or her lifetime.

In community property states the survivor takes at least one-half of all community property even though the testator attempts to will the survivor's share to another. In North and South Dakota, the spouse apparently has no right of election.

In the following chart illustrating the Spouse's Right of Election, the shares which may be taken as against the Will are outlined. Where an intestate share is allowed, the spouse inherits the same share that would have passed if there was no Will. Limitations on the share taken by election are included in states where they exist.

Dower or Curtesy as used here denotes the share a husband or wife would take, as provided in the table "Dower, Curtesy and Statutory Substitutions" and only indicates that the survivor takes the present statutory equivalent of Dower or Curtesy.

Spouse's Right of Election

State	Election by Husband	Election by Wife	Limitation or Share Under the Right of Election. •Period for Filing Election
ALABAMA T. 16 §§ 18, 19	No	Yes	Intestate share; if no children or descendants limited to $50,000. •Within 6 months after probate.

State	Election by Hus-band	Wife	Limitation or Share Under the Right of Election. •Period for Filing Election
ARKANSAS	Yes, if Will executed prior to marriage	Yes	Intestate share. •Within 1 month after expiration for filing
COLORADO Ch. 176 §37	Yes(1)	Yes(1)	One-half of entire estate. •Within 6 months after probate.
CONNECTICUT §7309	Yes	Yes	One-third of estate for life. •Within 2 months after expiration for filing claims.
DELAWARE §§3541, 3767, 3771, 3774	Yes		Life estate in all real property.
		Yes	Life estate in one-third of real property. •No fixed time.
DISTRICT OF COLUMBIA §18-211	Yes	Yes	Intestate share. •Within 6 months after administration granted.
FLORIDA §§731.34, 731.35	No	Yes.	Dower and one-third of all personal property. •Within 9 months after first publication of notice to creditors.
GEORGIA §31-103	No	Yes	Dower. •No fixed period.
ILLINOIS §§3-168, 3-169	Yes	Yes	If all children survive one-third of entire estate; if none survive one-half of entire estate. •Within 10 months after probate.
INDIANA §§6-2332 to 2336	Yes	Yes	Intestate share. •Within 6 months after probate.

State	Election by Hus-band	Wife	Limitation or Share Under the Right of Election. •Period for Filing Election
IOWA §636.22	Yes	Yes	Intestate share. •Within 60 days after probate or 6 months after notice of admission to probate.
KANSAS §59-2233	Yes	Yes	Intestate share. •Within 6 months after purobate(2).
KENTUCKY §392.080	Yes	Yes	Intestate share. •Within 1 year after probate.
MAINE Ch. 156 §14	Yes	Yes	Intestate share, limited to ½ of the estate. •Within 6 months after probate.
MARYLAND §§324, 327, 328 Art. 93	Yes	Yes	Dower or intestate share in real property and up to ½ of personal property. •Within 30 days after expiration of notice to creditors.
MASSACHUSETTS Ch. 191 §15	Yes	Yes	Intestate share limited to $10,000 plus income of excess for life. •Within 6 months after probate.
MICHIGAN §702.69	No	Yes	Intestate share; ½ of realty absolutely and ½ subject to legacies; personal property up to $5,000 and half of remainder. •Within 60 days after entry of order closing estate to claims.
MINNESOTA §525.212	Yes	Yes	Intestate share limited to ½ of entire estate. •Within 6 months after probate.

State	Election by Hus-band	Wife	Limitation orShare Under the Right of Election. •Period for Filing Election
MISSISSIPPI §668	Yes	Yes	Intestate share limited to ½ of entire estate(3). •Within 6 months after probate.
MISSOURI §§469.020, 469.100, 469.150	Yes	Yes	Intestate share. •Within 12 months after probate.
MONTANA §§22-107, 22-108, 22-109	No	Yes	Dower and intestate share of personal property(4). •Within 1 year after probate.
NEBRASKA §§3-107, 3-108	Yes	Yes	Intestate share. •Within 1 year after issuance of letters testamentary.
NEW HAMPSHIRE Ch. 359 §§10 to 14 inc.	Yes	Yes	Dower or curtesy plus one-third personal property if issue survive; if no issue $7,500 plus ½ remainder(5). •Within 1 year after death of testator.
NEW JERSEY T A3 c. 37 §§1, 2	Yes	Yes	Dower; Curtesy. •Within 6 months after probate.
NEW YORK D.E.L. §18	Yes	Yes	Intestate share limited to ½ of net estate. •Within 6 months after issuance of letters testamentary or letters of administration with Will annexed.
NORTH CAROLINA §§30-1, 30-2	No(6)	Yes	Intestate share. •Within 6 months after probate.
OHIO §10504-55	Yes	Yes	Intestate share limited to ½ of estate. •Within 1 month after service of citation to elect, if no citation is-

State	Election by Husband	Election by Wife	Limitation or Share Under the Right of Election. •Period for Filing Election
			sued within 9 months after appointment of executor or administrator.
OKLAHOMA T. 84 §44	Yes	Yes	Intestate share(7). •No fixed period.
OREGON §§17-113, 17-401; L. 1949 ch. 457 L. 1951 ch. 386	Yes	Yes	Dower or curtesy in real property plus an undivided one-fourth interest in personal property. •Real property: within year after death. Personal property: within 90 days after probate.
PENNSYLVANIA T. 20 §§180.8, 180.11	Yes	Yes	Intestate share. •Within 1 year after probate.
RHODE ISLAND Ch. 566 §§12, 21	Yes	Yes	Dower or curtesy. •Within 6 months after probate.
SOUTH CAROLINA 154 S.C. 64		Yes	Dower. •Prior to distribution of estate.
TENNESSEE §§8358, 8359, 8360	Yes	Yes	Dower or curtesy plus one-third of personal property if no child or not more than two survive; a child's part of personal property if more than two children survive. •Within 9 months after probate of will.
UTAH §§74-4-3, 74-4-4	No	Yes	Dower(8). •Within months after probate.
VERMONT §§3031, 3041		Yes	Dower or curtesy. •Within 8 months after probate.

State	Election by Hus-band	Election by Wife	Limitation or Share Under the Right of Election •Period for Filing Election
VIRGINIA §§64-13, 64-16, 64-23, 64-32	Yes	Yes	Dower or curtesy and intestate share in personal property up to one-half. •Within 1 year after death or probate.
WEST VIRGINIA §§4091, 4103	Yes	Yes	Dower or curtesy and one-third of the personal property. •Within 8 months after death.
WISCONSIN §§233.13, 233.14	No	Yes	Dower and up to one-third of the personal property. •Within 1 year after probate.
WYOMING §6-301	Yes	Yes	Intestate share of entire estate, limited to ¼ of children survive; ½ if no children survive. •Within 6 months after probate.

Footnotes

(1) Survivor may elect if testator attempts to Will away more than one half of the estate.

(2) If Will admitted to probate after June 30, 1951 survivor elects to take under intestate laws; if Will admitted prior to that date survivor must elect to take under Will, failure to so elect results in inheritance of intestate share.

(3) If the surviving spouse has separate property amounting to more than a one-fifth share of the estate, the survivor can only elect to take the difference between the seperate property and the share entitled under the election (§670).

(4) Widow may take one-half of realty absolutely, in lieu of dower, if no issue survive decedent.

(5) Survivor may waive dower or curtesy and take in lieu thereof, one-third of realty if issue survive; $7,500 plus one-half of excess if no issue survive.

(6) Surviving husband takes curtesy (§52-16).

(7) Survivor may will away half the property not acquired by joint industry during the marriage.

(8) Widow presumed to take distributive share unless she elects to take under the Will.

EFFECT OF DIVORCE, SEPARATION AND ANNULMENT: a. **Divorce:** A decree of absolute divorce terminates the marital relationship and deprives each spouse of any right to inherit any property from the other under the laws of intestacy. The divorce decree must be final. An interlocutory decree which requires that a period of time must elapse before the decree is final does not affect the inheritance rights of either spouse.

b. **Separation:** Where a husband and wife are living apart at the time that one of them dies, the survivor is not precluded from inheriting from the deceased spouse. This rule does not necessarily apply where one spouse abandons the other without just cause. The separation of husband and wife, whether or not judicially decreed, does not dissolve the marriage. A husband and wife may enter into a separation agreement, in most jurisdictions, and release to each other any rights of inheritance which may accrue. Where such a valid contract is entered into, the surviving spouse will be barred from inheriting from the estate of the decedent. A separation agreement which is subsequently abrogated by a reconciliation of husband and wife, does not prevent either spouse from sharing in the estate of the other.

c. **Annulment:** An annulment is a judicial declaration that a voidable marriage no longer exists; therefore neither party has any rights of inheritance in the estate of the other. If the marriage is voidable but no annulment was obtained, the parties will inherit from each other as husband and wife. If a marriage is void, the relationship of husband and wife never existed, and no right to share in each other's estate as husband and wife would exist.

INHERITANCE (by state)

ALABAMA **Real Property:** If there are no children, or descendants, and no parent, brother, sister or descendants of deceased brothers or sisters, all real property is inherited by the surviving husband or wife (T. 16 §1). In any case, the surviving husband receives a life estate in all real property owned by the wife at her death (T. 16 §12). The surviving wife shares in the real property by her dower right.

Personal Property: (a) Wife's Share—If no children survive the decedent the wife takes all; if survived by one child she takes one-half; if the decedent is survived by two, three or four children the wife receives a child's share; if five or more children survive, the wife receives one-fifth (T. 16 §10). If the separate property owned by the wife, at her husband's death is equal to or exceeds her share of the estate, she is barred from receiving any part of the estate (T. 16 §42); if her separate property is less than her share, her inheritance is reduced by the amount of her separate property (T. 16 §43). (b) Husband's Share —One-half of all the personal property (T. 16 §12).

ARIZONA **Community Property:** Upon the death of the husband or wife one-half of the community property shall go to the survivor. If the decedent is not survived by descendants, the surviving spouse inherits all the community property (§39-109).

Separate Property: If the decedent is survived by children or descendants, the spouse inherits one-third of the personal estate and takes a life estate in one-third of the real property. If the decedent is survived by a parent but no descendants the spouse inherits the entire personal estate and one-half of the real property. The surviving spouse inherits the entire estate where the decedent is not survived by descendants nor parents (§39-102).

ARKANSAS In addition to dower and curtesy the surviving spouse inherits one-third of the personal estate (§61-202). If no descendants survive the decedent, the spouse inherits one-half of the entire estate; part of which is subject to the right of creditors (§61-206, 228). If there be no children or their descendants, parents nor their descendants or any paternal or maternal kindred, the surviving spouse inherits the entire estate (§61-107).

CALIFORNIA **Community Property:** Upon the death of husband or wife, one-half of the community property goes to the survivor. If the other half is not disposed of by Will, it goes to the survivor (Prob. C. §201).

Separate Property: The surviving spouse inherits as follows—One-half of the entire estate if the decedent leaves one child or the issue of a deceased child; one-third, if the decedent leaves more than one child, or one child and the issue of one or more deceased children (Prob. C §221). The spouse takes one-half, if the decedent leaves no issue but is survived by either parent, brothers or sisters or their descendants (Prob. C. §223). The spouse inherits the entire estate if neither issue, parent, brother, sister, nor descendant of deceased brother or sister, survive the decedent (Prob. C. §224).

COLORADO The surviving spouse inherits one-half of the estate if the decedent is survived by children or their descendants; if no children or descendants of any child survive, the surviving spouse inherits the entire estate (ch. 176 §1).

CONNECTICUT The surviving spouse inherits one-third of the estate if the decedent is survived by children or descendants of deceased children. If the decedent is survived by a parent but no children or their representatives, the spouse inherits the whole estate up to $5,000, and one-half of the balance. The spouse inherits the entire estate if the decedent is survived by no children or representatives of children and no parent (§7309 as amend. L. 1951 P.A. 372).

DELAWARE In addition to dower and curtesy, the surviving spouse inherits as follows: **Real Property:** If the decedent leaves no heirs or next of kin surviving, the surviving spouse inherits all real property (§3731). **Personal Property:** The spouse inherits one-third of the personal property, if the decedent is survived by children or their descendants; the surviving spouse inherits all personal property if no children nor descendants survive (§3847).

DISTRICT OF COLUMBIA **Real Property:** The surviving spouse takes dower or curtesy in real property. The surviving spouse inherits all real property if the decedent is survived by no children, or descendants, parent, brother, sister or descendants of deceased brothers or sisters (§18-101). **Personal Property:** The surviving spouse inherits one-third of all personal property if decedent is survived by a child or descendants (§18-703). If the decedent is survived by no child or descendants but by either parent, and brother, sister or children of deceased brothers or sisters, the spouse inherits one-half. If the decedent is survived by none of the above mentioned, the spouse inherits all personal property.

FLORIDA The surviving spouse inherits a child's share of the entire estate if the decedent is survived by lineal descendants. If no lineal descendants survive the decedent, the surviving spouse inherits the entire estate (§731.23). The widow must elect to take her dower share as against her statutory share as a surviving spouse.

GEORGIA The surviving spouse inherits a child's share of the entire estate if the decedent is survived by children or their descendants; however, if there are more than five shares, the widow is entitled to one-fifth. The surviving spouse inherits the entire estate if the decedent leaves no children or descendants (§113-901). The widow must elect between dower and her distributive share in the real property of the estate. The right of election does not affect her inheritance of personal property.

IDAHO The surviving spouse inherits the following share of the entire estate; one-third, if the decedent is survived by two children or one child and issue of a deceased child or issue of two or more deceased children; one-half, if the decedent is survived by one child or issue of one deceased child or father or mother. The surviving spouse inherits the entire estate if the decedent is survived by neither issue or parent (§14-103).

ILLINOIS The surviving spouse takes the following

share of real and personal property; one-third if the decedent is survived by descendants; all personal property and one-half of the real property if the decedent is survived by no issue but parents, brother or sister or their descendants. The surviving spouse inherits the entire estate where decedent was not survived by descendants, parent, brother, sister or descendants of brothers and sisters (ch. 3 §162). The surviving spouse is required to elect between a dower interest in real property, and the share as outlined above. The spouse takes a distributive share of real property in which dower was not perfected.

INDIANA **Real Property:** The widow inherits one-half of the real property if decedent is survived by one child or descendant (§6-2314). If the decedent is survived by more than one child or descendant, the widow merits one-third of the real property, provided, that if the value of the real estate exceeds $10,000, the wido wtakes one-fourth as against creditors and if the value exceeds $20,000, she takes one-fifth as against creditors (§6-2313). The surviving husband inherits one-third of the real property if issue survive the decedent (§6-2321).

Personal Property: The widow inherits a child's share of the personal property, but not less than one-third, if the decedent is survived by children or descendants (§6-2320). The husband inherits one-third of the personal property if decedent is survived by issue (§-2322).

The surviving spouse inherits three-fourths of the entire estate if the decedent is survived by mother or father, but no child (§-2323). The entire estate passes to the surviving spouse if the decedent died leaving no child or parent (§6-2324).

IOWA In addition to dower or curtesy, the surviving spouse inherits the whole estate up to $15,000 and one-half of the excess if no issue survive the decedent (§636.32). The surviving spouse inherits the entire estate if the decedent leaves no issue, no parent nor heirs of any parent (§§636.40, 636.41).

KANSAS: In addition to dower or curtesy, the surviving spouse inherits one-half of the entire estate if the decedent is survived by a child or children or issue of a previously deceased child or children. The surviving spouse inherits the entire estate if the decedent was survived by no child or children or issue of a previously deceased child (§59-504).

KENTUCKY In addition to dower or curtesy, the surviving spouse inherits one-half of all personal property (§392.020). The survivor inherits the entire estate if the decedent is survived by neither paternal or maternal kindred (§391.010).

LOUISIANA **Community Property:** Upon the death of either spouse, one-half of the community property belongs to the survivor. The survivor takes one-half of community property undisposed of by Will if the decedent is survived by either mother or father but no descendants (C.C. 915). The survivor takes all undisposed community property if the decedent is survived by neither father, mother nor descendants (C.C. 915). The widow takes a usufruct (i. e., the use of real property) in a child's share if left with a child. The interest ceases when a second marriage is contracted (C.C. 916). **Separate Property:** The surviving spouse inherits all separate property if decedent left no lawful descendants, ascendants or collateral relatives; provided that the widower is so entitled only when the wife, in addition to above, leaves no natural child, or children duly acknowledged by her (C.C. 924).

MAINE: The surviving spouse inherits one-third of the estate if the decedent is survived by issue. If the decedent leaves no issue the survivor inherits one-half of the estate, provided, however, that if they were living together at death, the survivor takes $5,000 and one-half of the remainder of the estate. If no kindred survive, the survivor takes the entire estate (c. 156 §1). Dower and curtesy have been abolished; however, the one-third interest of the survivor in real property attaches to all real property owned during the marriage, which interest was not conveyed, released or barred.

MARYLAND Surviving spouse inherits an intestate share of real property unless an election to take dower or curtesy is made within six months after death (art. 46, §§1, 3). The surviving spouse inherits the following share of real property (if no election is made) and personal property: One-third, if decedent is survived by a child, children or descendants of a predeceased child or children (art. 93, §130). One-half if decedent is survived by a parent or parents, but no issue (art. 93, §131). The survivor inherits the whole estate up to $2,000 and one-half of the excess, if decedent is survived by a brother, sister or child of a deceased brother or sister, and no issue or parent (art. 93, §131). If the decedent is survived by none of the above mentioned, the survivor inherits the entire estate (art. 93, §129).

MASSACHUSETTS The surviving spouse inherits an intestate share of the estate unless an election to take dower or curtesy is made within six months after the date of the administrator's or executor's bond (ch. 189, §1). The survivor's intestate share is as follows: One-third of the estate if the decedent is survived by issue; $10,000 and one-half of the excess if kindred but no issue survive the decedent. If no kindred survive, the survivor inherits the entire estate (ch. 190, §1).

MICHIGAN The widow inherits an intestate share of the decedent's real property unless she elects to take dower within 60 days after the entry of order closing estate to claims (§702-70). The surviving spouse inherits the following intestate share of real and personal property; One-third of the estate if the children or issue of a deceased child or children survive the decedent; one-half of the estate if one child or issue of one deceased child survive the decedent. The surviving husband inherits one-half of the estate if no issue but a parent, brother, sister or children of a deceased brother or sister survive the decedent. If the decedent is survived by a parent, brothers, sisters or children of deceased brothers or sisters the widow inherits $3,000 and one-half of the balance of the estate. If no issue, parent, brother, sister or children of a deceased brother or sister survive the decedent, the surviving spouse inherits the entire estate (§702.93).

MINNESOTA The surviving spouse inherits one-third of the estate if more than one child or one child and issue of a deceased child or issue of two or more deceased children survive the decedent. If the decedent is survived by one child or the issue of one deceased child, the surviving spouse inherits one-half of the estate. If no issue or descendants survive the decedent, the survivor inherits the entire estate (§525.16). The surviving spouse takes the above-mentioned proportionate interest in all real property of which the decedent, while married to such spouse, we seized or possessed, to the disposition whereof such survivor shall not have consented in writing (§525.16).

MISSISSIPPI If children or their descendants survive the decedent, the surviving spouse inherits a child's share. If no children or descendants survive the decedent, the survivor inherits the entire estate (§§470, 472).

MISSOURI The surviving spouse inherits, in addition to dower or curtesy, a child's share of the personal property, if the decedent dies leaving a child, children or other descendants (§469.070). When the husband shall die without any child or other descendants his widow shall be entitled: (1) to all the real and personal estate which came to the husband in right of the marriage and all personal property, and to all the personal property which came to his possession with the written assent of the wife not subject to his debts; (2) to one-half of the real and personal estate belonging to the husband at the time of his death, absolutely, subject to the payment of the husband's debts (§469.090). When a wife shall dies without any child or other descendants, her widower shall be entitled to one-half of the real and personal estate belonging to the wife at the time of her death absolutely, subject to the payment of the wife's debts (§469.130). The surviving spouse may elect to take a child's share in real property, in lieu of dower, if the decedent is survived by children or descendants (§§469.-020, 469.080). The surviving spouse inherits the entire estatre, if the decedent is survived by neither child or descendant, parent, brother,sister or descendants of deceased brothers or sisters (§469.010).

MONTANA The widow takes dower in addition to her rights as heir under intestacy (28 Mont. 37). The surviving spouse inherits one-third of the estate, if the decedent is survived by more than one child or one child and issue of a deceased child or issue of more than one deceased child. If the decedent is survived by one child or the lawful issue of one child, the surviving spouse inherits one-half of the estate. If the decedent leaves no issue, entire estate goes to the surviving husband or wife (§91-403).

NEBRASKA The surviving spouse who is the parent of all children of the decedent inherits as follows: One-third of the estate if two or more children or one child and issue of one deceased child or issue of two or more deceased children survive the decedent. One-half if one child or issue of one deceased child survive the decedent. The survivor who is not the parent of all children of the deceased inherits one-fourth of the estate if one or more children or issue of one or more deceased children survive the decedent. The survivor inherits one-half of the estate if the decedent is survived by blood relatives and the entire estate, if none survive (§30-101).

The surviving spouse takes the above proportionate share in all real estate which the deceased owned at anytime during the marriage and not conveyed by the husband and wife, subject to the debts of the decedent (§30-101).

NEVADA **Community Property:** The surviving husband is entitled to all of the community property except that if the husband abandons his wife, he is only entitled to one-half (§3395.01). The surviving wife is entitled to one-half of the community property; if the decedent is not survived by children, the widow takes all, subject to any testamentary disposition over one-half (§3395.02).

Separate Property: The surviving spouse inherits the following share, subject to the decedent's debts: One-third, if more than one child or one child and descendants of one deceased child or descendants of two or more deceased children survive the decedent. The survivor inherits one-half, if one child, descendants of deceased child, parent, brother, sister or issue of a deceased brother or sister survive the decedent. If none of the last mentioned relatives survive, the spouse inherits all separate property (§982.-297).

NEW HAMPSHIRE **Real Property:** The widow takes her dower share unless it is waived, in which case the following intestate share is inherited: One-third if the decedent is survived by issue. If no issue survive the decedent, the widow inherits $10,000 and one-half of the excess (ch. 359, §11, Amend. L. 1951 ch. 29). The surviving husband takes his curtesy share unless it is waived, in which case he inherits one-third if issue, by him, survive. The surviving husband takes a life estate in one-third of all real property if issue by the wife and not by the widower survive and he takes no estate by the curtesy. The widower inherits $10,000 and one-half of the excess, if no issue survive (ch. 359, §11, Amend. L. 1951 ch. 29).

Personal Property: In addition to an inheritance in real property, the surviving spouse inherits one-third of all personal property if issue survive the decedent. The survivor inherits $10,000 and one-half of the excess if no issue survive (ch. 359, §§10, 12; Amend. L. 1951 ch. 29).

NEW JERSEY In addition to dower or curtesy, the surviving spouse inherits the following share: One-third of all personal property if the decedent is survived by children or descendants (T. 3A §4-2). If the decedent is not survived by children or descendants, the surviving spouse inherits the entire estate (T. 3A §4-3).

NEW MEXICO **Community Property:** Upon the death of the wife, the entire community property belongs to the husband (§31-108). Upon the death of the husband one-half of the community property goes to the surviving wife and the other half is subject to the testamentary disposition of the husband; in the absence of such testamentary disposition the wife takes one-fourth if issue survive the decedent; and all, if no issue survive (§31-108). **Separate Property:** The surviving spouse inherits one-fourth of all separate property if issue survive the decedent (§31-110). If no issue survive, the survivor inherits the whole estate (§31-113).

NEW YORK The surviving spouse inherits one-third of the entire estate if children or descendants survive the decedent. If the decedent is survived by a parent but no issue, the survivor takes $5,000 and one-half of the excess. If the decedent is survived by neither issue nor parent but by brothers, sisters or their descendants, the survivor takes $10,000 and one-half of the excess. The surviving spouse inherits the entire estate if the decedent is survived by neither children, descendants, parents, brothers, sister, niece or nephew (D.E.L. §83).

NORTH CAROLINA The surviving spouse takes dower or curtesy in real property. Personal property is distributed as follows: **Widow**—If the decedent is survived by one child or descendants of a deceased child the widow inherits one-half of the personal property. If more than one child or one child and the issue of one or more deceased children or issue of two or more deceased children survive the decedent, the widow inherits a child's share. If no issue but next of kin survive, the widow inherits $10,000 and one-half of the remainder. The widow inherits all personal property if no issue nor next of kin survive. **Husband**—One-half of the personal property is inherited by the husband where the decedent is survived by one child or descendants of a deceased child. If more than one child or one child and the issue of one or more deceased children or issue of two or more deceased children survive the decedent, the husband inherits a child's share. Where no children or descendants survive, the husband inherits all the personal property (§29-149).

When a husband or wife shall die leaving no heirs surviving, the surviving spouse inherits all real and personal property of the estate (§29-1, Rule 8).

NORTH DAKOTA The surviving spouse inherits one-third of the entire estate if the decedent is survived by more than one child or one child and the lawful issue of one or more deceased children. If the decedent is survived by one child or the lawful issue of one deceased child, the surviving spouse takes one-half of the estate. If the decedent is not survived by issue the surviving spouse inherits $15,000 and one-half of the excess if either parent survive the decedent. If the decedent leaves no issue or parent and the estate does not exceed $50,000 the whole thereof goes to the surviving spouse. If the decedent is not survived by issue or parent but leaves brothers, sisters or children of deceased brothers or sisters the spouse takes $25,000 and one-half of the excess. If the decedent is survived by neither issue, parent, brothers, sisters nor children of deceased brothers or sisters, the whole estate goes to the surviving spouse (§56-0104).

OHIO The surviving husband or wife takes dower only in those lands which were conveyed or incumbered during the lifetime of both, without the consent of the other spouse. There is no vested dower in lands owned by the decedent at his death. In lieu of such dower interest as terminates and is barred, pursuant to the statutes, the surviving spouse is entitled to the intestate share provided by the laws of inheritance (§10502-1).

The surviving spouse inherits the following intestate share: If there be a spouse and one child or its descendants, surviving, one-half to the surviving spouse. If there be a spouse and more than one child or their descendants, one-third to the surviving spouse. If there be no children or descendants but parents surviving, the spouse inherits three-fourths. If no children or their descendants nor parent survive, the surviving spouse inherits the entire estate (§10503-4).

OKLAHOMA The surviving spouse inherits one-half of the entire estate if the decedent is survived by one child or the issue of one deceased child. If the decedent is survived by more than one child or one child and the issue of one deceased child or issue of two or more deceased children, the spouse takes one-third. However, if the decedent was married more than once, the spouse at death takes only a child's share with living children and issue of deceased children in that property which was not acquired during the marriage. If no issue but a parent, brother or sister survive the decedent, the surviving spouse inherits one-half. However, the survivor inherits all property which was acquired during the marriage by the joint industry of husband and wife, if the decedent is not survived by issue. The surviving spouse takes the entire estate if neither issue, parent, brother or sister survive the decedent (84, §213).

OREGON The surviving spouse takes dower or curtesy in real property; if the decedent is not survived by lineal descendants, the survivor inherits all real property (§16-601). The spouse inherits one-half of all personal property if issue survive; all personal property if no issue survive the decedent (§16-102).

PENNSYLVANIA The surviving spouse inherits one-third of the entire estate if the decedent is survived by more than one child or one child and the issue of a deceased child or issue of more than one deceased child. If the decedent is survived by one child or the issue of one deceased child the survivor inherits one-half of the excess if no issue survive the decedent. The surviving spouse inherits all of the estate if the decedent is survived by no issue, parent, brother, sister, child of a brother or sister, grandparent, uncle or aunt (T. 20, §1.2). The wife takes her proportionate interstate share in all real property which her husband owned at his death or which was conveyed by him without her joining in the conveyance (T. 20, §1.5(A).

RHODE ISLAND In addition to dower or curtesy in real property, the surviving spouse takes one-half of the personal property if the decedent is survived by issue (ch. 567, §9). If no issue survive the decedent, the survivor takes $3,000 and one-half of personal property and a life estate in all real property (ch. 567, §§4, 9). If the decedent is survived by neither maternal nor paternal kindred, the surviving spouse takes the entire estate (ch. 567, §4).

SOUTH CAROLINA The widow takes dower unless she accepts her distributive share of the estate which, if accepted, is in lieu of and is in bar of dower. If the widow forfeits her dower she shall also forfeit her intestate share of her husband's real property (§§19-57, 151).

Subject to the exceptions above, the surviving spouse inherits the following share of all real and personal property: One-half if the decedent is survived by one child or descendants of a deceased child; one-third if the decedent is survived by more than one child or their descendants. The surviving spouse inherits one-half of the estate if decedent is survived by no children or issue but was survived by a parent or other ancestor, brother, sister, nephew or niece, of either whole or half blood. The survivor inherits the entire estate if none of the above mentioned survive the decedent (§19-52).

SOUTH DAKOTA If the decedent leaves a surviving spouse and more than one child or one child and the issue of a deceased child or the issue of two or more deceased children, the survivor inherits one-third of the estate. If one child or the issue of a deceased child survive the decedent, the surviving spouse inherits one-half of the estate. The spouse inherits $20,000 and one-half of the excess, if decedent is survived by no issue but a parent, brother or sister or descendants of deceased brothers and sisters. If the decedent leaves a surviving husband or wife and no issue, and no parent nor brother, nor sister, the whole estate shall go to the surviving husband or wife (§56.0104).

TENNESSEE In addition to dower or curtesy, the surviving spouse takes the following share: **Personal Property:** If decedent is survived by children or descendants the surviving spouse inherits a child's share of all personal property. If no children or descendants survive, the surviving spouse inherits all of the personal estate (§8389). **Real Property:** If the decedent leaves no heirs at law capable of inheriting real estate, it passes to the surviving spouse (§8382).

TEXAS **Community Property:** On the death of either husband or wife, all community property passes to the survivor, if the decedent is survived by neither children or descendants. If the decedent is survived by any children or descendants, the surviving spouse takes one half of the community property (§2578). **Separate Property:** If the deceased leaves a child, children, or descendants, the surviving husband or wife takes one-third of the personal estate and a life estate in one-third of real property. If no children or descendants survive the decedent, the spouse inherits all of the personal property and one-half of all real property absolutely. If the deceased has neither issue, parent, brothers, sisters nor their descendants surviving, the entire estate passes to the surviving spouse (§2571).

UTAH The widow takes a dower interest in real property. The share which is inherited as surviving spouse includes her dower interest, and is not in addition to dower (§74-4-3).

The surviving spouse inherits one-third of all real and personal property if the decedent is survived by one child or the issue of one deceased child. If more than one child or one child and the issue of a deceased child or issue of more than one deceased child survive the decedent, the spouse inherits one-third of the estate. The surviving spouse takes the whole estate up to $25,000, exclusive of debts and expenses, and one-half of the excess, if no issue but a parent, brother, sister or children or grand-children of a deceased brother or sister survive the decedent. If none of the above mentioned survive the decedent, the spouse inherits the entire estate.

VERMONT The surviving spouse takes dower or curtesy. Where the decedent is not survived by issue, the survivor takes an intestate share unless an election to take dower or curtesy is made within eight months after letters of administration are issued (§3031). The survivor inherits the whole estate up to $4,000 and one-half of the excess, if no issue survive. If the decedent has no kindred surviving, the spouse is entitled to the entire estate (§3042).

VIRGINIA The surviving spouse takes a dower or curtesy interest in real property. If the decedent is survived by a child or descendants the surviving spouse inherits one-third of the personal property. If no children or descendants survive, the surviving husband or wife is entitled to all personal property of the estate (§64-11).

WASHINGTON **Community Property:** Upon the death of either husband or wife, one half of the community property shall go to the survivor. If no testamentary disposition is made of the remainder, and no issue or descendants survive the decedent, the remainder of the community property passes to the surviving spouse. **Separate Property—Real Property:** The surviving spouse inherits one-third of all separate real property if more than one child or one child and the lawful issue of one or more deceased children or lawful issue of more than one deceased child survive the decedent. If the decedent is survived by one child or the lawful issue of a deceased child or parent, brother, sister, nephew or niece, the surviving spouse takes one-half of all separate real property. If none of the above mentioned survive, the survivor takes all real property

(§11.04.020). **Personal Property:** If the decedent left issue the surviving spouse inherits one-half of the personal property; if no issue survive, the spouse takes all personal property (§11.04.030).

WEST VIRGINIA **Real Property:** In addition to dower or curtesy, the surviving spouse takes the following share of real property: If the decedent leaves no issue but is survived by a parent and brothers, sisters or descendants of deceased brothers and sisters, the surviving spouse inherits one-fourth of the real property. If the decedent leaves no children or parent but is survived by a brother, sister or descendant of a deceased brother or sister, the surviving spouse takes one-half of the real property. If the decedent is survived by none of the above mentioned, the survivor inherits all real property (§4080). **Personal Property:** If the decedent is survived by issue, the survivor inherits one-third; if no issue survive, the surviving spouse inherits all personal property (§4089).

WISCONSIN The surviving spouse takes an intestate share in personal property in addition to dower or curtesy in real property. If one child or descendant of a deceased child survives the decedent, the surviving spouse inherits one-half of all personal property. In all other cases the spouse is entitled to one-third of the personal property. If no children or other lineal descendants survive the decedent, the surviving spouse inherits all real and personal property of the estate (§237.01).

WYOMING The surviving spouse inherits one-half of the entire estate, if the decedent is survived by children or descendants. If no descendants but a parent, brother or sister survive the decedent, the spouse takes the whole estate up to $20,000 and three-fourths of the excess. If there be none of the aforementioned relatives of the intestate, the surviving spouse inherits the entire estate (§6-2501).

Chapter IV

MARRIAGE AND DIVORCE

Marriage

Marriage has been defined as "the legal union for life of one man and one woman to discharge toward each other and toward the community the duties imposed by law on persons related as husband and wife."

How is the marital status created? The basic element of the agreement is "consent." Without it there can be no valid marriage. However, consent alone in many jurisdictions will not suffice to make the agreement valid. We must recall that the state is a party to the contract; that marriage is a social institution in which the state has an interest. The state may require that other conditions be met before it will recognize that a valid marriage exists.

Is is therefore possible for a marriage to take place by either of two methods:

(a) marriage based solely on the consent of the parties capable of entering into matrimony.

(b) upon the consent of the parties plus a ceremony duly solemnizing and recording such consent.

"COMMON LAW" MARRIAGE: Such a marriage—that is, a marriage without ceremony of any sort but where man and woman live together as man and wife and hold themselves out as such to the world—is recognized by court decisions in the following states and territories:

Alabama	**Ohio**
Alaska	**Oklahoma**
Colorado	**Pennsylvania**

Florida	Rhode Island
Georgia	South Carolina
Idaho	***South Dakota
Iowa	Texas
*Kansas	District of Columbia
***Montana	

They are recognized in:

California	—if entered into before 1895.
Indiana	—if entered into before January 1, 1958
Michigan	—if entered into before January 1, 1957
Minnesota	—if entered into prior to April 26, 1941
Missouri	—if entered into before April 4, 1956
Nebraska	—if entered into prior to March 31, 1921
Nevada	—if entered into prior to 1923
New Jersey	—if entered into prior to March 29, 1943
New York	—if entered into prior to December 1, 1939
Mississippi	—if entered into prior to April 29, 1933

They are prohibited by statute in the following States:

Arizona	New Mexico
Arkansas	North Carolina
California	North Dakota
Connecticut	Oregon
Delaware	Utah
Hawaii	Vermont
Illinois	Virginia
**Kentucky	West Virginia
Louisiana	Wisconsin
Maryland	Wyoming
Massachusetts	Puerto Rico
New Hampshire	

*Kansas	—But parties are punished for not obtaining a license
*Kentucky	—Common law marriage valid only for workmens Compensation law purposes
***Montana South Dakota	—But parties must record joint declaration of marriage

While common law marriages generally are recognized in Kansas, the parties are punished for disregarding the license provisions of the statute.

Some states, although prohibiting common law marriage to their own residents, will recognize as valid such marriages entered into in states where these marriages are deemed valid.

LICENSED MARRIAGE: This type is recognized in all states, and, as has just been pointed out, in most of the fifty states it is absolutely necessary to comply with certain requirements set out by state law regulating marriage in order to enter into a vaild marriage.

RESTRAINTS UPON MARRIAGE: Almost every state recognizes certain disabilities or legal impediments to marriage. The presence of these disabilities may make the purported marriage either absolutely **void** or merely **voidable.** A voidable marriage is valid until its validity is attacked in a court and a decree setting it aside is entered. However, no decree is generally necessary to set aside a void marriage since it never was valid.

Void marriages result from the following disabilities in most states.

1. A prior marriage is still existing (bigamous marriage).
2. The parties, either by birth or marriage are related to each other within certain prohibited degrees (incestuous marriages).
3. The parties, or either of them is an adjudged lunatic or idiot. In some states, the marriage of such persons is voidable but not void.

Voidable marriages generally require an action for annulment to set them aside and are the result of the disabilities set forth below to name but a few. In order to set aside a marriage, the party suffering from the disability or against whom fraud has been practised or force exerted must bring an action. In the case of an infant or an insane person, the action may be brought by his legal representative. The following disabilities may create a voidable marriage.

1. Either party is under the age of consent.
2. Either party lacked understanding necessary to consent to the marriage.

3. Either party was physically incapable of having intercourse.
4. Either party consented to the marriage through fraud, force or duress.

These disabilities must usually have existed at the time of the marriage ceremony in order to provide valid grounds for the annulment action.

1. Nonage

Where either or both parties are below the age of consent. The age of consent for common law marriages is fourteen for males and twelve for females. In the states where the legislature has enacted provisions governing marriage, the age of consent varies. Such conditions must be complied with in order to effect a valid marriage.

All states specify the ages below which persons may not marry and the ages at which they may marry, with parental consent. In most states, the age limits may be disregarded, in the best interests of the minors. The pregnancy of the girl is generally considered a good reason for the relaxation of the rule.

2. Consanguinity.

Where the parties are by birth or marriage within certain prohibited degrees of relationship as specified in the laws of the state where marriage took place, no valid marriage can occur.

ALL states prohibit marriages between a person and his or her:

(a) mother or father
(b) daughter or son
(c) grandmother or grandfather
(d) granddaughter or grandson
(e) aunt or uncle
(f) sister or brother
(g) niece or nephew

3. Mixed Marriages.

Many states, by statute, prohibit mixed marriages (miscegenation)—marriages between white persons and Negroes, Orientals or Indians. Generally such prohibition is effective to the third generation inclusive with regard to the descendants of Negroes, Orientals or Indians, and many state legislatures have specifically stated that marriage between a white person and a person of ⅛ Negro blood is prohibited. These marriages, if performed in violation of the statute are usually void. Interestingly enough, at least one state (California) has declared unconstitutional a law which prohibits interracial marriages.

Creating The Marital Status

Assuming, however, that the persons who wish to marry are free from any legal restraints, what does the law require of them to make the marriage "legal."

It has already been indicated that in most of the states it is absolutely necessary to comply with certain specific statutory regulations in order to enter into a valid marriage. These laws provide:

1. Requirements concerning physical examinations.
2. Minimum waiting periods, if any.
3. Time for performance of ceremony.
4. Who may perform the marriage ceremony.
5. The words, if any, necessary to solemnize a marriage ceremany.

1. PHYSICAL EXAMINATIONS.

While in almost all states, marriage by one infected with venereal disease is forbidden, many states prescribe, in addition, that applicants for a marriage license must present affidavits or medical certificates showing them to be free from venereal infection at the time of the application for the license.*

Some states also set a limit upon the period which may expire between the date of the physical examination and the date of the application for a marriage license.

2. WAITING PERIODS . . . TIME OF PERFORMANCE OF CEREMONY

Assume now that the prospective husband and wife have

* Some jurisdictions will waive the requirement of physical examination for "good cause shown" where the court so orders (e.g., where the prospective wife is pregnant at the time of application for a license to marry.)

passed the physical examination and have presented the medical certificate with their application for a license within the period set by law. A license to marry will now be issued.

Note that the parties are still NOT married.

The license must be delivered to the person who will perform the ceremony. Many jurisdictions require the ceremony to be performed within a specific period of time after the license has been issued. A ceremony which is performed after this statutory period has expired will be invalid.

Aside from the maximum limitation, some states require

MINIMUM WAITING PERIODS. These states insist upon a minimum waiting period between the time that the license to marry has been issued and the ceremony. It should be noted that some states have longer waiting periods for non-residents than for residents.

Many jurisdictions provide for a waiting period between the time that the application for the license is made and the day on which it is issued.

Another waiting period required by some states is that no ceremony may be performed for a stated time after the seriological test is made.

Let us review the provisions in one state to help us understand them.

In New York, before John can validly marry Jane he must do the following:

1. Obtain a certificate signed by a duly licensed physician, stating that both he and Jane have been given a seriological test and found free from infection.
2. Present this certificate WITHIN 30 DAYS after the date of the examination along with the application for a license to marry.
3. After receiving a license—deliver it WITHIN 60 DAYS to the person who will perform the ceremony However, in New York, the ceremony may not take place WITHIN 24 HOURS after the license has

been issued or WITHIN 3 DAYS from the date of the physical examination.

3. CEREMONY

It should be pointed out that in only three states,—Delaware, Maryland and West Virginia,—is a religious ceremony required, but that in all states any duly ordained clergyman of any religion or sect is empowered to perform the marriage ceremony. In most states numerous other officials, such as judges of various courts, justice of the peace, mayors, recorders, city and police magistrates, are also designated to perform marriages. Practically all states have enacted provisions for the keeping of a record of marriages. Marriage licenses are issued by various officials, County Clerk, Probate Judge, Recorder, Registrar of Births, Justice of Peace, etc., depending upon individual state regulations. Various states have a special provision for solemnizing of marriages in Quaker and Baha'i faiths.

As a general rule, the state laws do not require any specific type of ceremony or the words to be spoken therein. So long as the parties solemnly declare that they take each other as husband and wife and do so in the presence of the individual performing the ceremony, then the ceremony is legal. The requirement for witnesses also varies in the several states and territories.

Annulment

An action to annul a marriage is a legal proceeding based on the theory that no valid marriage was ever contracted. **It must generally be founded upon a cause which existed at the time of the marriage.**

The grounds for annulment are fixed in most states by statute, although in some states annulments have been granted without any statutory provision therefor. It should be remembered, therefore, that the statutory grounds listed in the materials which follow, are by no means exclusive. Courts of "equity" have broad powers and may grant relief for causes which are not listed in the statutes.

The reader should keep in mind that "fraud" as a ground for annulment may include many possible fact patterns. A detailed discussion is beyond the scope of this book. The facts should be discussed with an attorney and his advice sought. It can be indicated in general terms, however, that the following examples of fraud (to name but a few) have at times successfully been the grounds for an annulment:

a. Concealment of a previous marriage or divorce;
b. Financial misrepresentation;
c. Concealment of pregnancy;
d. Misrepresentations as to chastity;
e. Concealment of disease;
f. Misrepresentation of character;
f. Refusal to have children (the agreement to raise a family is implicit in the marriage relationship);
h. Promise to have a religious ceremony after the civil ceremony.

Once the grounds for an action of annulment have been discovered, the injured party must act within a reasonable time to have the marriage set aside. If the injured party thereafter voluntarily cohabits with the guilty spouse the suit will be barred.

Grounds for marriage annulment

NONAGE

Thirty-two States grant an annulment when one or both parties are below the age of consent to marriage or have not attained the statutory age required to contract a valid marriage:

Alabama
Arkansas
California
Colorado
District of Columbia
Florida
Idaho
Illinois
Indiana
Iowa
Kansas
Louisiana
Maine
Michigan
Minnesota
Mississippi
Missouri
Nebraska
New Jersey
New Mexico
New York
North Carolina
North Dakota
Oklahoma
Oregon
Rhode Island
Tennessee
Vermont
Washington
West Virginia
Wisconsin
Wyoming

Four additional States make nonage a ground for annulment when the marriage is entered into without parental consent: Kentucky, Montana, Nevada, South Dakota.

MENTAL INCAPACITY

Thirty States permit annulment of marriage on the ground of mental incapacity. The degree of such incapacity is usually prescribed by law, and the statutes vary considerably:

Alabama	Maine	Oklahoma
Arkansas	Michigan	Oregon
California	Minnesota	South Dakota
Delaware	Mississippi	Tennessee
District of Columbia	Missouri	Texas
Florida	Montana	Vermont
Idaho	Nevada	Virginia
Indiana	New York	Washington
Iowa	North Carolina	West Virginia
Kansas	North Dakota	Wisconsin

FRAUD

Twenty-three States permit annulment of marriages that have been procured by fraud:

Alabama	Indiana	North Dakota
Arkansas	Kentucky	Oregon
California	Michigan	South Dakota
Delaware	Minnesota	Vermont
District of Columbia	Montana	Washington
Florida	Nebraska	Wisconsin
Georgia	Nevada	Wyoming
Idaho	New York	

PROHIBITED DEGREES OF KINSHIP

Twenty-two States provide for annulment if the marriage is incestuous or the parties are within prohibited degress of kinship:

Alabama	Minnesota	Oregon
California	Mississippi	Pennsylvania
Delaware	Missouri	Vermont
Iowa	Nebraska	Virginia
Louisiana	New Jersey	West Virginia
Maine	New Mexico	Wisconsin
Maryland	North Carolina	
Michigan	North Dakota	

DURESS OR FORCE

Twenty-one States grant annulment of marriage to persons whose consent has been induced by duress or force:

Arkansas	Louisiana	Oregon
California	Michigan	South Dakota
Delaware	Minnesota	Tennessee
District of Columbia	Montana	Vermont
Florida	Nebraska	Washington
Idaho	New York	Wisconsin
Kentucky	North Dakota	Wyoming

PHYSICAL INCAPACITY

Physical incapacity to enter into the marriage relationship is a ground for annulment in 19 States:

Arkansas	Montana	Texas
California	Nebraska	Vermont
Delaware	New Jersey	Virginia
District of Columbia	New York	West Virginia
Idaho	North Carolina	Wisconsin
Iowa	North Dakota	
Michigan	South Dakota	

INTERRACIAL MARRIAGES

Seven States permit annulment of certain interracial marriages:

Louisiana	Missouri	Virginia
Mississippi	Nebraska	West Virginia
	Oregon	

The California law prohibiting marriages between white persons and members of certain racial groups was invalidated in 1948 because it was violative of the due process and equal protection clauses of the fourteenth amendment to the United States Constitution.

FORMER UNDIVORCED SPOUSE LIVING

Annulment may be granted in 19 States on the ground that one of the parties had at the time of the marriage a living undivorced spouse:

Delaware	Minnesota	South Dakota
Idaho	Missouri	Tennessee
Iowa	Montana	Vermont
Louisiana	New Jersey	Virginia
Maine	North Dakota	West Virginia
Maryland	Oregon	Wisconsin
	Pennsylvania	

It should be noted that marriages entered into when one of the parties has a living undivorced spouse are void ab initio. Formal annulment is generally provided for in order that the record may be clarified.

OTHER GROUNDS

Maine and Maryland permit a spouse whose husband or wife has been sentenced to life imprisonment to obtain an annulment. New York and North Dakota grant annulment if a husband or wife is absent for 5 years preceding the filing of the complaint and the other spouse has no knowledge of his whereabouts. In Oklahoma, if one of the parties has been divorced for less than 6 months at the time of the marriage, the other party may secure an annulment.

MISCELLANEOUS

Several states have laws declaring that cohabitation of the parties ratifies marriages which might be annulled because of nonage, fraud, duress, or force.

Illinois (1951) enacted legislation declaring that no insane or mentally ill person is capable of contracting marriage.

California (1951), North Carolina (1951), Oregon (1951), and South Carolina (1951) enacted legislation preserving the legitimacy of children born of voidable or bigamous marriages.

Divorce

The topic of Divorce is complicated. At no time should a person attempt to solve his individual problems without the aid of an attorney once he or she is involved in a suit of divorce.

The rights and liabilities of the spouses may vary depending in which state the action is brought and whether it is defended or not. They may even depend on whether there has been a personal appearance by the defendant or the plaintiff. No attempt will be made within this booklet to discuss these problems in detail. The purpose is merely to acquaint the reader with some of the possible pitfalls.

RESIDENCE REQUIREMENTS: All states have a minimum period during which person is required to be a continuous resident before a divorce may be obtained. This requirement is primarily to discourage (or encourage) residents of foreign states from shopping around for an easy jurisdiction in which to start a divorce action. Different rules may apply where the marriage was solemnized in the state; or where both parties were always residents of the state, etc.

Most of the states also have the same or similar time residence requirements in connection with annulment and separation suits.

It should also be indicated that these residence requirements may not necessarily apply where the ground for the divorce is "insanity subsequent to the marriage." Because of the unusual nature of the grounds, many states require proof of residence for the same period that the insanity must exist before it is considered as a cause for an absolute divorce.

In some states the residence requirements differ according to the ground for the action and whether the cause arose in or out of the state.

Most states today credit time served in the armed forces toward the residence period required.

The form of complaint in a divorce action is farily well standardized. It must state date and place of the marriage; names and ages of the children, if any; a statement to the effect that the plaintiff is a resident of the state in which the action is brought; the facts on which the cause of action is based; that the statutory period of limitation has not elapsed since the discovery by the plaintiff of the cause of action against the defendant; that the plaintiff has not forgiven the cause of action against the defendant and generally a statement to the effect that the plaintiff has not voluntarily cohabited with the defendant since the discovery of the cause of action; that no decree of divorce has been obtained by the defendant against the plaintiff, and that no other action for divorce between the parties is pending. In a divorce action where the wife is the plaintiff and there are no children, it is sometimes desirable to ask that she be permitted to resume her maiden name. Then, at the court hearing, the plaintiff is generally asked what her maiden name was and if she wants to resume it and if so a provision is included in the decree to that effect. The complaint must be sworn to as to the truth thereof of the facts stated by the plaintiff.

While unquestionably divorce procedure could be further simplified, even though there are fifty different divorce laws in the United States, a great deal of simplification has been accomplished in the last hundred years. The first divorces in the United States required the passage of a special law for each one by the state legislature.

The courts still insist that a divorce suit must represent a contest, although a large percentage of divorces are amicable and have been arranged between the parties. Nevertheless, in the eyes of the law, before any decree may be entered, the court must be satisfied that it has jurisdiction of the parties and that there has been a genuinely contested divorce action. In view of present day procedure this attitude seems positively absurd and hypocritical.

The courts of New York recognize only one ground for divorce—adultery. When a divorce decree has been duly obtained in New York it is of course recognized by every New York court. Likewise, where a divorce is duly obtained outside of New York, where both parties are actual bona fide residents of the state or county where such divorce is obtained, New York will recognize such a divorce as valid. But what about divorce decrees rendered outside of the state and where only one of the parties establishes a foreign residence? It is understandable that persons will seek relief where the courts are most amenable to divorce actions. Will New York recognize the validity of these "Foreign Divorce Decrees"?

FOREIGN DIVORCES: The Supreme Court of the United States has been called upon to rule on the validity of foreign divorces many times within the past few years. The question is in many respects still open to dispute. Some general principle of law, however, may be suggested as a result of these restrictions.

Assume that John and Jane were married in state X and are both residents of that state. They live happily for a while and then fall into marital difficulties. Jane leaves John, moves to state Y and starts an action for divorce. She is granted a divorce decree by the court of state Y and returns to state X. Will state X recognize this decree of its sister state? This will depend on the following circumstances:

1. Did Jane establish a legal domicile (residence) in State Y?
2. Was John personally served with the summons in State Y or did he appear in court or did he appear by an attorney or did he receive notice of the divorce action only by publication?

If both parties submitted to the jurisdiction of state Y and the court there found that the plaintiff had established a bona fide domicile, then the divorce decree of state Y must be recognized in state X.

If, however, the plaintiff did not make personal service of the summons on the defendant in the state but served notice on him only by publication then, even though the court of state Y found that bona fide domicile had been established, its decree is not conclusive in state X. The finding of domicile by the court in state Y is entitled to prima facie weight in the court of a sister state but does not prevent relitigation of the question there. The decree of divorce of state Y under these circumstances may be collaterally attacked in the courts of a sister state.

As a general rule, then, the law may be stated as follows:

1. Where both parties have appeared in the divorce

action in state Y, the validity of its decree may not be collaterally attacked in any other state.

2. Where there has been no appearance by the defendant in the court of state Y, its divorce decree is not conclusive in state X. Persons who seek the advantages of a quick and easy divorce must remember the risk involved.
3. Where alimony, custody, counsel fees and other factors are involved, the problem is further complicated.

A recent case illustrates the latter point (*Estin v. Estin*, 334 U. S. 541 (1948). After five years of marriage the husband abandoned his wife in 1942. In 1943 the wife sought and was awarded (husband appearing personally in the action) a decree of separation in New York. The decree included an award of alimony. The husband then went to Nevada and instituted an action for divorce on grounds which were recognized in Nevada. The court granted the divorce decree but the wife was not personally served with the summons nor did she appear at the trial. The divorce decree made no provision for alimony. After the divorce, the husband ceased paying alimony which was still due under the separation decree of the New York court. The wife now sued the husband in New York for arrears in alimony. The husband defended on the grounds that the Nevada divorce decree ended his obligation to make further alimony payments. The New York court granted the wife a judgment of alimony arrears. This decree was subsequently affirmed in the Supreme Court of the United States.

The rationale of the case is as follows:

The Nevada divorce decree was recognized in New York so far as the marital status of the parties was concerned. New York recognized that they were now legally divorced.

But the alimony provision which had originally been awarded in the New York separation decree was a "property right" and the Nevada court could not adjudicate the wife's rights in regard to such property rights unless it had personal jurisdiction over her.

In effect then, the foreign decree was recognized by the New York court in some respects and denied validity in others.

MEXICAN DIVORCES: Before concluding the subject of divorce a word should be said regarding so-called Mexican divorces. Very often parties who cannot obtain a divorce for one reason or another in their own states try to break the bonds of matrimony by obtaining a decree in Mexico. Such divorces are frequently subject to attack.

Separation

A Separation, or as it is sometimes called, a limited divorce differs from both annulment and divorce in important respects. It is limited in the sense that the parties are still married to each other. They are merely separated from bed and board but not from the bonds of matrimony.

Suit for separation may in most states be brought by either the husband or the wife. In all cases, however, the party bringing the suit must be the party not at fault. A separation suit is generally brought for permanent separate maintenance and support of the wife or the wife and children. The most common grounds are desertion or cruel and inhuman treatment. In some states the action is one which may be instituted only by the wife. Suit for a separation does not bar the complaining party from later bringing an action for absolute divorce on the same or upon additional grounds. After the parties enter into separation agreements which are filed in court at the time suit for separation is begun, such agreements are, if properly drawn, recognized by the court and in many cases, included in the decree of separation.

The separation decree sanctions the refusal of the wife to cohabit. The decree or judgment of separation may later be revoked in most of the states by either of two methods (1) By the joint application of the parties to the court upon a reconciliation, or (2) by the parties voluntarily cohabiting with each other without any formal court proceedings for revocation of the separation decree.

Grounds for Divorce (by subject)

ADULTERY—all jurisdictions

DESERTION, ABSENCE, OR ABANDONMENT

Alabama
Alaska
Arizona
California
Colorado
Connecticut
Delaware
District of Columbia
Florida
Georgia
Hawaii
Idaho
Illinois
Indiana
Iowa
Kansas
Kentucky
Louisiana
Maine
Maryland
Massachusetts
Michigan
Minnesota
Mississippi
Missouri
Montana
Nebraska
Nevada
New Hampshire
New Jersey
New Mexico
North Dakota
Ohio
Oregon
Pennsylvania
Rhode Island
South Carolina
South Dakota
Tennessee
Texas
Utah
Vermont
Virginia
Washington
West Virginia
Wisconsin
Wyoming

CONVICTION FOR FELONY

Alabama
Alaska
Arizona
Arkansas
California
Colorado
Connecticut
Delaware
District of Columbia
Georgia
Hawaii
Idaho
Illinois
Indiana
Iowa
Kansas
Kentucky
Louisiana
Maryland
Massachusetts
Michigan
Minnesota
Mississippi
Missouri
Montana
Nebraska
Nevada
New Hampshire
New Mexico
North Carolina
North Dakota
Ohio
Oklahoma
Oregon
Pennsylvania
Rhode Island
South Dakota
Tennessee
Texas
Utah
Vermont
Virginia
Washington
West Virginia
Wisconsin
Wyoming

CRUELTY

Alaska
Arkansas
California
Colorado
Connecticut
Louisiana
Maine
Maryland
Massachusetts
Minnesota
Oklahoma
Oregon
Pennsylvania
Rhode Island
South Carolina

CRUELTY (Continued)

Delaware
Florida
Georgia
Hawaii
Idaho
Illinois
Indiana
Iowa
Kansas
Kentucky
Mississippi
Missouri
Montana
Nabraska
Nevada
New Hampshire
New Jersey
New Mexico
North Dakota
Ohio
South Dakota
Tennessee
Texas
Utah
Vermont
Washington
West Virginia
Wisconsin
Wyoming

HABITUAL DRUNKENNESS

Alabama
Alaska
Arizona
Arkansas
California
Colorado
Connecticut
Delaware
Florida
Georgia
Hawaii
Idaho
Illinois
Indiana
Iowa
Kansas
Kentucky
Louisiana
Maine
Massachusetts
Michigan
Minnesota
Mississippi
Missorui
Montana
Nebraska
Nevada
New Hampshire
New Mexico
North Dakota
Ohio
Oklahoma
Oregon
Rhode Island
South Carolina
South Dakota
Tennessee
Utah
Washington
West Virginia
Wisconsin
Wyoming

IMPOTENCE

Alabama
Alaska
Arizona
Arkansas
Colorado
Florida
Georgia
Illinois
Indiana
Kansas
Kentucky
Maine
Maryland
Massachusetts
Michigan
Minnesota
Mississippi
Missouri
Nebraska
Nevada
New Hampshire
New Mexico
Ohio
Oklahoma
Oregon
Pennsylvania
Rhode Island
Tennessee
Utah
Virginia
Washington
Wisconsin
Wyoming

IDIOCY OR INSANITY

Alabama
Alaska
Kansas
Kentucky
Maryland
South Dakota
Texas
Utah

IDIOCY OR INSANITY (Continued)

Arkansas	Indiana	North Dakota
California	Minnesota	Oklahoma
Colorado	Mississippi	Oregon
Connecticut	Montana	Vermont
Delaware	Nebraska	Washington
Georgia	Nevada	Wyoming
Hawaii	New Mexico	
Idaho	North Carolina	

NONSUPPORT

Either spouse

Arkansas	North Dakota	Utah

Wife only

Alabama	Indiana	Rhode Island
Alaska	Maine	Tennessee
Arizona	Massachusetts	Vermont
Colorado	Nebraska	Washington
Delaware	Nevada	Wisconsin
Hawaii	New Hampshire	Wyoming
Idaho	New Mexico	

VOLUNTARY SEPARATION

Alabama	Louisiana	Texas
Arizona	Maryland	Utah
Arkansas	Minnesota	Vermont
District of Columbia	Nevada	Washington
	New Hampshire	Wisconsin
Idaho	North Carolina	Wyoming
Kentucky	Rhode Island	

WIFE'S UNDISCLOSED PREGNANCY BY ANOTHER MAN AT TIME OF MARRIAGE

Alabama	Kentucky	Oklahoma
Arizona	Mississippi	Tennessee
Georgia	Missouri	Virginia
Iowa	New Mexico	Wyoming
Kansas	North Carolina	

VIOLENCE

Alabama	Colorado	Louisiana
Alaska	Illinois	Missouri
Arizona	Iowa	Tennessee
Arkansas	Kentucky	West Virginia

PRIOR UNDISSOLVED MARRIAGE

Arkansas	Illinois	Missouri
Colorado	Kansas	Ohio
Delaware	Mississippi	Oklahoma
Florida		

FRAUD OR COERCION TO OBTAIN CONSENT

Connecticut	Kentucky	Pennsylvania
Georgia	Ohio	Washington
Kansas	Oklahoma	

DRUG ADDICTION

Alabama	Maine	Rhode Island
Colorado	Massachusetts	West Virginia
Hawaii	Mississippi	

INDIGNITIES

Either spouse

Arkansas	Oregon	Washington
Hawaii	Pennsylvania	Wyoming
Missouri		

Wife only

Tennessee

WILFUL NEGLECT

Either spouse

Alaska	Kansas	Oklahoma
California	Ohio	South Dakota
Idaho		

Wife only

Montana

SEPARATION UNDER A DECREE OF LIMITED DIVORCE

District of Columbia	Louisiana	North Dakota
	Minnesota	Virginia

RELATIONSHIP BETWEEN PROHIBITED DEGREES OF KINSHIP

Florida	Georgia	Pennsylvania
	Mississippi	

WANT OF AGE OR LEGAL UNDERSTANDING

Delaware	Mississippi	Washington
Georgia		

DISEASE

Delaware (epilepsy)	Illinois (venereal)	Kentucky (loathsome)

FAILURE TO COHABIT

Kentucky	New Hampshire	North Dakota

FRAUDELANT DIVORCE OBTAINED IN ANOTHER JURISDICTION

Florida	Michigan	Ohio

CRIME AGAINST NATURE

Alabama	North Carolina

INCOMPATIBILITY

Florida	New Mexico

LEGALLY VOID OR VOIDABLE MARRIAGE

Maryland	Rhode Island

VAGRANCY

Wife only

Missouri	Wyoming

GROSS MISBEHAVIOR

Rhode Island

SODOMY AND BUGGERY

Virginia

UNDISCLOSED PRACTICE OF PROSTITUTION BY WIFE BEFORE MARRIAGE

Virginia

UNCHASTE CONDUCT OF WIFE, THOUGH ADULTERY NOT PROVED

Kentucky

GROUNDS FOR DIVORCE

By State

( ) Years required for condition to exist

ALABAMA: Impotence, adultery, desertion (1), conviction for felony (7), unnatural behavior, habitual drunkenness, husband's use of drugs, husband's failure to support wife (2), idiocy or insanity (5), wife pregnant at time of marriage, violent temper or behavior, husband and wife living apart (2).

ARIZONA: Impotence, adultery, desertion (1), conviction for felony (1), habitual drunkenness, wife pregnant at time of marriage, violent temper or behavior, husband and wife living apart (5), non-support by husband (1), extreme cruelty, indignities.

ARKANSAS: Impotence, adultery, desertion (1), conviction for felony, habitual drunkenness (1), idiocy or insanity (3), husband and wife living apart (3), extreme cruelty, prior marriage exists, indignities.

CALIFORNIA: Adultery, desertion (1), conviction for felony, habitual drunkennes (1), idiocy or insanity (3), extreme cruelty, wilful neglect (1).

COLORADO: Impotence, adultery, desertion (1), conviction for felony, habitual drunkenness (1), habitual use of drugs (1), idiocy or insanity (5), non-support by husband (1), extreme cruelty, prior marriage exists.

CONNECTICUT: Adultery, desertion (3), conviction for felony, habitual drunkenness, idiocy or inanity (5), extreme cruelty, wilful neglect (3), fraud, disappearance (7).

DELAWARE: Adultery, desertion (2), conviction for felony (2) habitual drunkenness (2), idiocy or insanity (5), non-support by husband, extreme cruelty, prior marriage exists, epilepy (5). Plaintiff under age of consent, unless marriage confirmed after reaching the age of consent.

DISTRICT OF COLUMBIA: Adultery, desertion (2), conviction for felony (2), husband and wife living apart; upon application of the innocent party, a decree of divorce from bed and board which resulted in separation of parties for 2 years; may become an absolute divorce.

FLORIDA: Impotence, adultery, desertion (1), habitual drunkenness, violent temper or behavior, extreme cruelty, prior marriage exists, related within prohibited degree (incest), divorce out of the state by other party.

GEORGIA: Impotence, adultery, desertion (1), conviction for felony (2), habitual drunkenness, wife pregnant at time of marriage, extreme cruelty, fraud, related within prohibited degree, (incest), mental incapacity, force or duress.

IDAHO: Adultery, desertion (1), conviction for felony, habitual drunkenness (1), idiocy or insanity (3), husband and wife living apart (5), non-support by husband (1), extreme cruelty, wilful neglect.

ILLINOIS: Impotence, adultery, desertion (1), conviction for felony, habitual drunkenness (2), extreme cruelty, prior marriage exists, venereal disease, attempt on life of other.

INDIANA: Impotence, adultery, disertion (2), conviction for felony, habitual drunkenness, idiocy or insanity (5), non-support by husband (2), extreme cruelty.

IOWA: Adultery, desertion (2), conviction for felony, habitual drunkenness, extreme cruelty, attempt on life of other, wife pregnant at time of marriage unless husband had an illegitimate child living at time of marriage, unknown to wife.

KANSAS: Impotence, adultery, desertion (1), habitual

drunkenness, idiocy or insanity (5), wife pregnant at time of marriage, extreme cruelty, prior marriage exists, wilful neglect, fraud, conviction of a felony.

KENTUCKY: Impotence, adultery, desertion (1), conviction for felony, habitual drunkenness (1), idiocy or insanity (5), wife pregnant at time of marriage, violent temper or behavior, husband and wife living apart (5), non-support by husband, extreme cruelty (6 months), wilful neglect, fraud, force or duress, venereal disease, attempt on life of other, wife's unchastity, indignitities, leprosy or other loathsome disease. Also for malformation preventing sexual intercourse and for joining sect believing cohabitation unlawful.

LOUISIANA: Adultery, desertion, conviction for felony, habitual drunkennes, violent temper or behavior, husband and wife living apart (2), extreme cruelty, attempt on life of other, public defamation of other. Except in cases where either spouse has been sentenced to an infamous punishment or was guilty of adultery, no divorce shall be granted unless a judgment of separation from bed and board shall have been rendered and one year shall have expired and reconciliation shall not have taken place.

MAINE: Impotence, adultery, desertion (3), habitual drunkenness, habitual use of drugs, non-support by husband, extreme cruelty, wilful neglect.

MARYLAND: Impotence, adultery, desertion (condition must exist for 18 months), conviction for felony (3), idiocy or insanity (3), husband and wife living apart (3). Also "for any cause which would render the marriage null and void."

MASSACHUSETTS: Impotence, adultery, desertion (3), conviction for felony (5), habitual drunkenness, habitual use of drugs, non-support by husband, extreme cruelty, wilful neglect.

MICHIGAN: Impotence, adultery, desertion (2), conviction for felony (3), habitual drunkenness, violent temper or behavior, non-support by husband, extreme cruelty, wilful neglect, divorce out of the state by other party.

MINNESOTA: Impotence, adultery, desertion (1), conviction for felony, habitual drunkenness (1), idiocy or insanity (5), husband and wife living apart (5), unless under decree of separate maintenance, then (3); extreme cruelty.

MISSISSIPPI: Impotence, adultery, desertion (1), conviction for felony, habitual drunkenness, habitual use of drugs, idiocy or insanity (3), wife pregnant at time of marriage, extreme cruelty, prior marriage exists, related within prohibited degree (incest), mental incapacity.

MISSOURI: Impotence, adultery, desertion (1), conviction for felony, habitual drunkenness (1), wife pregnant at time of marriage, extreme cruelty, prior marriage exists, indignities, husband's vagrancy.

MONTANA: Adultery, desertion (1), conviction for felony, habitual drunkenness (1), idiocy or insanity (5), violent temper or behavior, non-support by husband, extreme cruelty (1), wilful neglect (1), attempt on life of other, public defamation of other. (See p. 68.)

NEBRASKA: Impotence, adultery, desertion (2), conviction for felony (3), habitual drunkenness, idiocy or insanity (5), violent temper or behavior, non-support by husband, extreme cruelty, wilful neglect.

NEVADA: Impotence, adultery, desertion (1), conviction for felony, habitual drunkenness, idiocy or insanity (2), husband and wife living apart (3), non-support by husband (1), extreme cruelty, wilful neglect (1).

NEW HAMPSHIRE: Impotence, adultery, desertion (3), conviction for felony (1), habitual drunkenness (3), non-support by husband (3), extreme cruelty, disappearance (3). Also for joining religious sect believing cohabitation unlawful and for refusing to cohabit; husband's departure from the United States with intention of becoming a citizen of a foreign country and failure to provide support for wife; wife's wilful absence from state for 10 years without husband's consent.

NEW JERSEY: Adultery, desertion (2), extreme cruelty.

NEW MEXICO: Impotence, adultery, desertion, conviction for felony, habitual drunkenness, idiocy or insanity (5), wife pregnant at time of marriage, non-support by husband, extreme cruelty. Also for incompatibility.

NEW YORK: Adultery. Life imprisonment and absence without tidings for 5 years are grounds for dissolution of marriage by order of the court.

NORTH CAROLINA: Impotence, adultery, unnatural behavior, idiocy or insanity (5), wife pregnant at time of marriage, husband and wife living apart (2).

NORTH DAKOTA: Adultery, desertion (1), conviction for felony, habitual drunkenness (1), idiocy or insanity (5), non-support by husband (1), extreme cruelty, wilful neglect (1).

OHIO: Impotence, adultery, desertion (3), conviction for felony, habitual drunkenness (3), non-support by husband, extreme cruelty, prior marriage exists, wilful neglect, fraud, divorce out of the state by other party.

OKLAHOMA: Impotence, adultery, desertion (1), conviction for felony, habitual drunkenness, idiocy or insanity (5), wife pregnant at time of marriage, non-support by husband, extreme cruelty, prior marriage exists, wilful neglect, fraud, incompatibility.

OREGON: Impotence, adultery, desertion (1), conviction for felony, habitual drunkenness (1), idiocy or insanity (5), extreme cruelty, indignities.

PENNSYLVANIA: Impotence, adultery, desertion (2), conviction for felony (2), extreme cruelty, prior marriage exists, fraud, related within prohibited degree (incest), force or duress, attempt on life of other, indignities.

RHODE ISLAND: Impotence, adultery, desertion (5), conviction of felony, habitual drunkenness, habitual use of drugs, husband and wife living apart (10), non-support by husband (1), extreme cruelty, prior marriage exists, wilful neglect, under age of consent, related within prohibited degree (incest). Divorces also decreed where marriage was originally void or voidable by law, or in case either party is for crime deemed civilly dead, or from absence or other circumstances may be presumed to be dead.

SOUTH CAROLINA: Adultery, desertion (1), physical cruelty, habitual drunkenness or drug addiction.

SOUTH DAKOTA: Adultery, desertion (1), conviction for felony, habitual drunkenness (1), idiocy or insanity (5), non-support by husband (1), extreme cruelty, wilful neglect (1).

TENNESSEE: Impotence, adultery, desertion (2), conviction for felony, unnatural behavior, habitual drunkenness, wife pregnant at time of marriage, violent temper or behavior, non-support by husband, extreme cruelty, prior marriage exists, wilful neglect, attempt on life of other, indignities. Also for refusal by wife to move to a new residence.

TEXAS: Adultery, desertion (3), conviction for felony, idiocy or insanity (5), violent temper or behavior, husband and wife living apart (7), extreme cruelty.

Statute: Tex. Civ. Stat. (Vernon, 1940), Art. 4629.

UTAH: Impotence, adultery, desertion (1), conviction for felony, habitual drunkenness, idiocy or insanity (5), husband and wife living apart (3), (under a decree of separate maintenance of any state), non-support by husband, extreme cruelty, wilful neglect.

VERMONT: Adultery or crimes against nature, desertion (3), conviction for felony (3), idiocy or insanity (5), husband and wife living apart (3), non-support by husband, extreme cruelty, wilful neglect, disappearance (7).

VIRGINIA: Impotence, adultery, desertion (1); indictment or conviction before marriage of infamous crime, for felony, wife pregnant at time of marriage, wife unknown to husband, prostitute before marriage.

WASHINGTON: Impotence, adultery, desertion (1), conviction for felony, habitual drunkenness, idiocy or insanity (5), husband and wife living apart (5), non-support by husband, extreme cruelty, wilful neglect, fraud, force or duress, indignities; lack of understanding.

WEST VIRGINIA: Adultery, desertion (2), conviction for felony, habitual drunkenness, habitual use of drugs, extreme cruelty, attempt on life of other, public dafamation of other.

WISCONSIN: Impotence, adultery, desertion (1), conviction for felony (3), habitual drunkenness (1), violent temper or behavior, husband and wife living apart (5), non-support by husband, extreme cruelty, wilful neglect.

WYOMING: Impotence, adutlery, desertion (1), conviction for felony, habitual drunkenness, idiocy or insanity (2), wife pregnant at time of marriage, husband and wife living apart (2), non-support by husband (1), extreme cruelty, wilful neglect (1), indignities, husband's vagrancy.

ALASKA: Impotence, adultery, desertion (1), conviction for felony, habitual drunkenness (1), idiocy or insanity (3), violent temper or behavior, non-support by husband (1), extreme cruelty, wilful neglect (1).

HAWAII: Adultery, desertion, (condition must exist for six months), conviction for felony, habitual drunkenness (1), habitual use of drugs (1), idiocy or insanity (3), non-support by husband, extreme cruelty, venereal disease, indignities, leprosy, or other loathsome disease.

Chapter V

TIPS TO THE LADIES

While this volume has concentrated on material basic to a woman's understanding of her place in society, this chapter is devoted to a few do's and don'ts of daily living. For the average woman, remaining essentially at home and plying her trade as home economist, is nevertheless the focal point of many relationships.

Safety first!

People who come on your premises other than as trespassers can hold you liable for injury to them resulting from your negligence, or even from something which the law assumes to be your negligence. This advice should apply: 1) Make sure that you have liability coverage with an insurance company; 2) Keep your property, both inside and out, in good, safe condition. In particular avoid situations that are "attractive nuisances" to youngsters.

Further in this connection, when a workman comes on your premises to do a job, ascertain that he carries liability insurance—protecting others against his negligence, and protecting his workmen against injury on your premises.

The "safety" rules apply as well to your car. Remember —when you transport the neighbor's children, you invite liability in the event of an accident. Make sure you are covered by insurance. If you are part of a pool or consistently pick up and carry other youngsters, work out with the other women an understanding that the risk of accident, for other than your own negligence, is not assumed.

Caveat Emptor!

Second to being a homemaker, the housewife is a consumer. But the law of the market place is that the buyer must beware! It is your obligation to see to it that what you receive is what you have bought. While fraud or misrepresentation puts the burden back on the merchant, in general, the duty to inspect goods and merchandise is on the buyer. This applies particularly to "as is" and "final" sales. Often, lack of care at the time of purchase creates dissatisfaction and controversy later. While most merchants—valuing their reputations—will take a reasonable view of a situation, they will not take responsibility for a change of mind or for damage to a product which was not pointed out at time of sale, or fairly soon thereafter. Department stores, more impersonal in the handling of these matters, frequently will go further than the smaller, local merchant—but no business concern will permit itself to be taken advantage of.

A more difficult area is contracting for work around the house. Particularly where this involves borrowing, no papers should be signed that would enable the contractor to have his money from the lending institution until the job is completed to your satisfaction. Once you have authorized the bank to pay, you have no recourse against either the contractor or the bank, except in legal proceedings. Payment is the leverage that you have in seeing to it that a job is done in accordance with your requirements. Don't pay until you get that kind of a job!

Bits and pieces!

If you hire a domestic on any kind of a regular basis—even once every week or once every two weeks, she is now covered by social security, and both you and she have to make a contribution to social security in her behalf. Failure to do this could create trouble for both of you, and you could find yourself one day with a heavy assessment to meet to bring her account up to date.

For you to be able to withdraw from the family bank account, you have to be one of the parties in a joint account. Many women will mistakenly draw a check, signing their own names, when the account is in the husband's name. The check will bounce! Other women will forge the husband's signature. Even when this practice is pursued with the husband's knowledge and consent, it can lead to problems—difficulty of identification of his correct signature and possibly, legal entanglements. If a wife and husband are to use a bank account interchangeably, it should be a joint and several account where both parties have the independent right to withdraw. Then the problem becomes only that of keeping each other informed as to what checks are written.

While cancelled checks and money order duplicates are adequate evidence that bills have been paid, where they are paid in cash, a signed receipt should always be required. Otherwise you can be put in the position of being dunned for a bill that you have already paid.

If you worry about the possibility of accidents happening to the children at school, most schoools today offer student accident policies. For a premium of $3 to $4 per year, you are covered for all kinds of injuries to the youngsters at school and traveling to and from school. While the policy can't prevent accidents, it can indemnify when they occur.

Practice to be a widow!

This is harsh advice, but to be taken seriously. Women outlive men in this country, and it is important for them to know how to carry on, once the husband is gone. Basic to this is a knowledge of his affairs and cooperation with him in ordering them.

What, for example, is your husband's life insurance coverage? Has he a planned life insurance program? Will the proceeds be paid in a lump sum or on a monthly income basis? While his social security will provide up to $250 per month for you and your children until they reach age 18, are you aware that thereafter, social security gives you no benefits until you reach age 62? This so-called "black-out period," generally hitting a widow in her forties is one of the most difficult problems a widowed housewife has to contend with. Planning now, together with the husband, can minimize its impact.

Do you and your husband have wills? Have you nominated guardians for the children? Does his will take full advantage of the marital deduction, i.e., leaving at least one-half of his estate to you, with the result that this portion is not subject to estate taxes? Do you have a family attorney to whom you can turn for advice as readily as you seek out your family doctor?

Is there an inventory of all of your and your husband's holdings? Can they be easily located? Is the ownership in the best form, as far as flexibility is concerned and as far as ultimate taxes and administration costs are concerned? Often, a trust will operate much more effectively than joint ownership of property. The possibility should be considered with your attorney.

If your husband is in business, have you worked out plans for the future of the business in the event of his death? If there are partners, is there a buy-and-sell arrangement that will pay you off for his share? If not, what protection have you as far as his interest in the business is concerned?

If your husband is an employee, are you familiar with all of the fringe benefits to which he may be entitled? Is there group life insurance? Is there a pension plan at his place of work? If he is a union member, are you familiar with the benefits to which he is entitled from the union welfare fund? All these things are important when, one day, you may have to face life without him, and to make a start at it, must at least know what he had, where it is, and how best it can be made to work for you and your family.

ACKNOWLEDGMENTS

Particularly helpful in the preparation of this volume has been a U.S. Department of Labor publication, "The Legal Status of Women in the United States of America." Published by the Women's Bureau, Alice K. Leopold, Director, it was issued in 1956 and reprinted in 1958. Likewise helpful was Mrs. Leopold's article, "The Legal Status of Women," which appeared in The Book of the States, 1960-61, published by The Council of State Governments.

Several prior Legal Almanacs have also contributed to the material herein, requiring adaptation to the woman's angle and interest. Especially useful were *Marriage and Divorce*, Legal Almanac No. 1, and Law of Inheritance, Legal Almanac No. 33.

INDEX